BEST PRACTICE FOR THE TOEIC® L&R TEST

–Intermediate–

TOEIC® L&R TEST への総合アプローチ
—Intermediate—

YOSHIZUKA Hiroshi

Graham Skerritt

Michael Schauerte

音声ファイルのダウンロード／ストリーミング

CDマーク表示がある箇所は、音声を弊社HPより無料でダウンロード／ストリーミングすることができます。下記URLの書籍詳細ページに音声ダウンロードアイコンがございますのでそちらから自習用音声としてご活用ください。

https://seibido.co.jp/ad646

BEST PRACTICE FOR THE TOEIC® L&R TEST
—Intermediate—

はしがき

　TOEIC (Test of English for International Communication) を作成している米国のETS (Educational Testing Service) によれば、英語はもはや世界の4人にひとりが使う言語になりました。今日のグローバル社会において英語は私たちにとって水や空気と同じく、使えて当たり前の存在になったと言っても過言ではありません。また、ETSはTOEICを「職場 (workplace) や日常生活 (everyday life) に必要な英語のコミュニケーションスキル」を測定するテストと言っています。ここで言う「職場」とはビジネスだけでなくあらゆる「職場」を意味しています。社会人ならどの「職場」であっても共通して登場するようなシチュエーションや語彙が試されています。決して特殊なビジネス英語が出題されるわけではありません。その意味で社会人を目指す学生にとって知っておくべき内容がたくさん含まれたテストになっています。

　皆さんにはTOEICの受験のために学習するだけでなく、グローバル人材の重要な要素のひとつとしての英語力を身に付ける、という意識で取り組んでいただきたいと思います。そして聞いたり読んだりして分かる、という受動的な学習に留まることなく、話したり書いたりできるようになるために、ぜひ、音読を繰り返したり、書写 (transcribe) をしたりという能動的な繰り返し学習を通じ、一生使える英語を身に付けていただきたいと思います。本書はTOEICスコア550～600を目標とする方々のために書かれています。本書が皆さんの目標達成のお役に立つことを心から願っています。

　本書の発刊に当たり、前作『BEST PRACTICE FOR THE TOEIC® LISTEING AND READING TEST−REVISED EDITION』をBasicからAdvancedまでのシリーズ三部作にすることをご提案いただいた成美堂の佐野英一郎氏、引き続き編集の労をお取りくださり随所にアドバイスをいただいた宍戸貢氏、そして今回から編集メンバーに加わっていただいた太田裕美氏、丁寧な校正をしてくださったBill Benfieldの各氏に改めて御礼申し上げます。

2021年秋
吉塚　弘
Graham Skerritt
Michael Schauerte

本書の構成と使い方

■全般：

・全UnitがRestaurantsやEntertainmentなどのトピック別の構成になっています。

・各Unitには、Part 1〜Part 7までの全てが収められています。

・各Partの問題は、Unit 1〜Unit 14へと出題頻度と重要度の観点から配置されています。

▶Warm up — Dictation Practice：

・リスニングセクションに入る前の耳慣らしです。

・音声は成美堂ホームページ （https://www.seibido.co.jp/ad646） よりダウンロードあるいはスマートフォンやタブレットでストリーミング再生してください。

・日本人にとって聞き取りにくい音の変化を学べるようになっています。聞き取りの際の注意点は、"Points to Dictate"にあります。

・Unitを追うごとに空所の数が増え、難易度が増します。

☞音声を聞き、空所部分を書き取ってください。音声は何度聞いても構いません。

▶頻出単語チェック！：

・各Unitのトピックに頻出し、当該Unitでも使用されている語句をチェックします。

・リスニングとリーディングの両セクションの最初のページにあります。

☞見出し語句と適切な意味（英語）を選びます。意味は本文で使われている意味が表示されています。

▶各Partの構成：

全Partに"Check Point!"があります。何を学ぶのか、どのような能力を身に付ければよいのかを明示しました。

LISTENING SECTION

- Part 1は、He, She, The man, The womanなどの頻出する主語と動詞を取り上げています。

- Part 2は、質問文に頻出する疑問詞を中心とした構成になっています。

- Part 3は、会話の内容や目的、誰と誰の会話かなどの概略を問う質

問文を例題の最初に取り上げています。2名の会話だけではなく3名の会話を聞いて解答する問題や、図表を見ながら解答する問題、話し手の意図を問う問題もUnit 10以降に採用しています。

- Part 4は、説明文の主旨や主題、目的などの概略を問う質問文を問題の最初に取り上げています。音声と印刷された図表の情報を関連づけて解答する質問と、話し手の意図を問う質問もUnit 10以降に採用しています。

☞ Warm up同様に音声は成美堂ホームページ (https://www.seibido.co.jp/ad646) よりダウンロードあるいはスマートフォンやタブレットでストリーミング再生してください。

▶Grammar Review：

- 文法項目を頻度順に復習します。

☞各項目の説明を読み、続く例題に取り組みましょう。

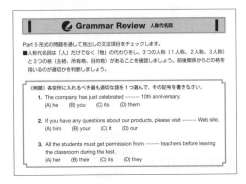

READING SECTION

- Part 5は、5つの問題のうち、最初の3つが文法問題、残り2つが語彙問題です。文法問題は前ページのGrammar Reviewで学んだ内容が問われています。語彙問題も頻度の高い品詞を取り上げています。

- Part 6は、3つの空所 (実際のテストでは4つ) のうち、2つは文法問題と語彙問題で、3つ目は文挿入問題です。

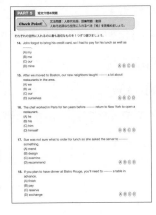

・Part 7は、出題頻度の高いEメールやメモ、手紙、広告文などを取り上げています。それぞれの説明文の主旨や主題、目的などの概略を問う質問文が問題の最初に出題されています。また、最近出題されるようになったテキストメッセージやオンラインチャット形式の問題や3つの文書を読んで解答する問題、さらに書き手の意図を問う質問や1文を挿入する文挿入問題を採用しています。

☞Part 5〜Part 7までは、目安の制限時間を設けて取り組みましょう。

Part 5 ---- 3分45秒（45秒@1問）

Part 6 ---- 2分30秒（50秒@1問）

Part 7 ---- 1分40秒（50秒@1問）←1つの文書

3分00秒（60秒@1問）←2つの文書

4分00秒（80秒@1問）←3つの文書

◎TOEIC必須複合名詞100

巻末付録として「必須複合名詞100」を付けました。知っている単語が2つ並ぶと知らない単語に変身してしまいます。リスニングの一瞬で聞こえたり、リーディングの一部に登場すると「何のこと？」となってそれ以降の音声が聞けなくなったり、読めなくなったりします。✔ボックスを付けておきましたので、知らないものがあったら必ず覚えましょう。

●TESTUDY **TESTUDY**

本書ではTESTUDY（=TEST+STUDY）という「e-learning+オンラインテスト」システムがご利用いただけます。

1. e-Learning：各Unitの復習ができます。（標準学習時間＝30分）

2. Unit Review：各Unitのリスニングセクションをベースにしたディクテーション問題です。（標準学習時間＝15分）

3. Extra Test：オンラインテストです。（標準学習時間＝50分）

☞全て教員の指示に従って学習・受験してください。

目 次

Restaurants

:: Warm up | **Dictation Practice** 1-02

それぞれの空所に入る語を、音声を聞いて書き入れてみましょう。

1. Can (   ) sit at that table?
2. This is (   ) favorite restaurant.
3. Can (   ) have a menu?
4. Please let (   ) know when you have decided.
5. Can you take (   ) order, please?
6. Do (   ) have any specials today?
7. Grilled chicken is (   ) favorite dish.
8. Everyone has almost finished (   ) meals except me.
9. Will you bring (   ) coffee after the meal?
10. Please give (   ) a receipt.

 Points to Dictate

まずは1語の聞き取りです。ここではすべて代名詞の例で、少し聞き取りにくいので注意しましょう。人称代名詞は前後関係があって使われます。誰のことを指すのかが明白なので弱く速く、さらに前後の音のつながりで多様に変化します。

 ✓ 頻出単語チェック! **Listening Section**

単語と意味を品詞に気をつけながら結びつけてみましょう。

1. cuisine (   )
2. diet [n.] (   )
3. cafeteria (   )
4. recommendation (   )
5. amazing (   )
6. server (   )
7. decide (   )
8. vegetarian (   )

a. very good
b. a self-service restaurant (often in an office or school)
c. a person who takes orders and brings food in a cafe or restaurant
d. a plan to not eat some foods (perhaps to lose weight)
e. a style of cooking
f. to choose
g. someone who does not eat meat
h. a suggestion

PART 1　写真描写問題

 1-03, 04

> **Check Point!**　1人の人物の動作について述べる例を見てみましょう。
> The man's cleaning the chair.

それぞれの写真について、4つの説明文の中から最も適切なものを1つずつ選びましょう。

1.

Ⓐ Ⓑ Ⓒ Ⓓ

2.

Ⓐ Ⓑ Ⓒ Ⓓ

PART 2　応答問題

 1-05-09

> **Check Point!**　最頻出の疑問詞 (What) で始まる質問文をチェックしましょう。
> What time does the restaurant open on Sundays?

それぞれの設問の応答として最も適切なものを1つずつ選びましょう。

3. Mark your answer on your answer sheet.　　　Ⓐ Ⓑ Ⓒ

4. Mark your answer on your answer sheet.　　　Ⓐ Ⓑ Ⓒ

5. Mark your answer on your answer sheet.　　　Ⓐ Ⓑ Ⓒ

6. Mark your answer on your answer sheet.　　　Ⓐ Ⓑ Ⓒ

7. Mark your answer on your answer sheet.　　　Ⓐ Ⓑ Ⓒ

 **PART 3** 会話問題 1-10, 11

Check Point! 「何について話し合われているのか」大きく捉えましょう。
What are the speakers discussing?

会話についての設問に対し、最も適切なものを1つずつ選びましょう。

8. What are the speakers discussing?
(A) The prices of the food
(B) The choices on the menu
(C) The taste of the food
(D) The service at the restaurant

9. What does the man want to do?
(A) Get some drinks
(B) Ask the chef for a
recommendation
(C) Look at the menu
(D) Decide what to order

10. What will the woman probably do next?
(A) Order the chicken
(B) Order the fish
(C) Order the steak
(D) Talk to the server

PART 4 説明文問題 1-12, 13

Check Point! 「話者は誰なのか」大きく捉えましょう。
Who is the speaker?

説明文についての設問に対し、最も適切なものを1つずつ選びましょう。

11. Who is the speaker?
(A) A customer
(B) A chef
(C) A server
(D) A reviewer

12. What does the man highly recommend?
(A) Goat cheese
(B) Baked salmon
(C) Vegetarian lasagna
(D) The choice of desserts

13. What will the man do soon?
(A) Take the orders
(B) Offer the salad
(C) Bake the bread
(D) Bring the menus

Part 5 形式の問題を通して見出しの文法項目をチェックします。

■人称代名詞は「人」だけでなく「物」の代わりをし、3つの人称（1人称、2人称、3人称）と3つの格（主格、所有格、目的格）があることを確認しましょう。前後関係からどの格を用いるのが適切かを判断しましょう。

《例題》各空所に入れるべき最も適切な語を1つ選んで、その記号を書きなさい。

1. The company has just celebrated ------- 10th anniversary.
   (A) he   (B) you   (C) its   (D) them

2. If you have any questions about our products, please visit ------- Web site.
   (A) him   (B) your   (C) it   (D) our

3. All the students must get permission from ------- teachers before leaving the classroom during the test.
   (A) her   (B) their   (C) its   (D) they

Reading Section

✔ 頻出単語チェック！ Reading Section

語句と意味を品詞に気をつけながら結びつけてみましょう。

1. chef (   )
2. convention (   )
3. in regard to (   )
4. fully booked (   )
5. go ahead (   )
6. instead (   )
7. review [n.] (   )
8. dish [n.] (   )

a. about
b. a large event for people who do a similar job
c. a person who makes food in a restaurant (often the manager of the kitchen)
d. to start to do something
e. having no available places for customers to use
f. an opinion about the good and bad points of something
g. as an alternative
h. a particular type of food that was made as part of a meal

PART 5 短文穴埋め問題

Check Point! 文法問題：人称代名詞、語彙問題：動詞
人称代名詞なら空所に入れるべき「格」を見極めましょう。

それぞれの空所に入れるのに最も適切なものを1つずつ選びましょう。

14. John forgot to bring his credit card, so I had to pay for his lunch as well as
-------.
(A) my
(B) me
(C) our
(D) mine   Ⓐ Ⓑ Ⓒ Ⓓ

15. After we moved to Boston, our new neighbors taught ------- a lot about
restaurants in the area.
(A) we
(B) us
(C) our
(D) ourselves   Ⓐ Ⓑ Ⓒ Ⓓ

16. The chef worked in Paris for ten years before ------- return to New York to open a
restaurant.
(A) he
(B) his
(C) him
(D) himself   Ⓐ Ⓑ Ⓒ Ⓓ

17. Sue was not sure what to order for lunch so she asked the server to -------
something.
(A) mend
(B) design
(C) examine
(D) recommend   Ⓐ Ⓑ Ⓒ Ⓓ

18. If you plan to have dinner at Bistro Rouge, you'll need to ------- a table in
advance.
(A) finish
(B) pay
(C) reserve
(D) exchange   Ⓐ Ⓑ Ⓒ Ⓓ

Check Point!　語彙問題：名詞
文章挿入問題：空所が文末なら結びとなる文を選びましょう。

それぞれの空所に入れるのに最も適切なものを1つずつ選びましょう。

To: Fred Hanson <fhanson@shiftnet.com>
From: Jane Richards <jrichards@shiftnet.com>
Date: March 8
Subject: Dinner reservations

Hi Fred,

I'm writing in regard to the client dinner that you asked me to arrange on the first night of the convention in Las Vegas next month. The Mexican restaurant that you ---**19.**--- in our discussion at the planning meeting is fully booked that night. But there is a similar restaurant nearby called Harry's Hacienda. Shall I go ahead and make a reservation there instead?

Another ---**20.**--- is to reserve a table at the French restaurant in the hotel next to the convention center. You said that the clients like Mexican food, but this restaurant has excellent reviews online, and I'm confident that the clients would enjoy it. When you have a chance, please let me know which place I should call. ---**21.**---.

Best regards,

Jane

---

19. (A) mention
(B) mentions
(C) mentioned
(D) mentioning

20. (A) place
(B) issue
(C) possibility
(D) condition

21. (A) I'm interested to hear how you like the restaurant.
(B) If possible, we should decide some time this week.
(C) As a result, I'll send some menus later today.
(D) Thank you for recommending this to me.

PART 7 読解問題

Check Point! E-mail（1つの文書）
差出人、受信者、件名などには常に目を通しましょう。

文章を読んで、それぞれの設問の答えとして最も適切なものを1つずつ選びましょう。

✉ **E-MAIL**

To:	Diane Wilson <diane-w@easymail.com>
From:	Gina Dennis <gdennis@connect-net.com>
Date:	August 4
Subject:	A new French restaurant

Hi Diane,

How are you?

I'm writing because I wanted to tell you about a great new French restaurant I went to last night – because I know you would like it too!

It's called Paris Bistro and it's on Morrison Street, near the sports center, so it's pretty easy to get to. It opened a couple of months ago and I've been wanting to try it for weeks.

Anyway, Doug and I went there last night and we loved it. First of all, the look of the place is great. They have these beautiful black and white photos of Paris on the walls. And the food was fantastic. I had chicken and Doug had seafood – and both dishes were excellent.

The only problem was that the restaurant was really busy so the service was a little slow – but we went on a Friday night, so it may be less busy during the week.

Anyway, you should try it!

Kind regards,

Gina

22. What is the purpose of the e-mail?
(A) To invite Diane to a restaurant
(B) To complain about a restaurant
(C) To ask Diane about a restaurant
(D) To recommend a restaurant

23. What is indicated about the restaurant?
(A) The food is a little expensive.
(B) The service is not quick enough.
(C) The decorations are not good.
(D) The location is pretty inconvenient.

7

Entertainment

Warm up | **Dictation Practice** 1-14

それぞれの空所に入る語を、音声を聞いて書き入れてみましょう。

1. Where (   ) the actor live?
2. I (   ) seen that movie three times.
3. She (   ) watch the horror movie by herself.
4. You should (   ) gone to the park with us.
5. I'll pick you up (   ) the theater.
6. The actress is (   ) Italy.
7. If you have (   ) questions, please ask one of the guides.
8. Brad (   ) Mary graduated from the same dance school.
9. (   ) you enjoy the performance?
10. (   ) you turn on the TV?

 Points to Dictate

前回の人称代名詞に続いて、助動詞、接続詞、前置詞などの「機能語」と呼ばれるものの聞き取りです。機能語は文章中で当然そこにあるべき語ですので、やはり弱く短く発話されます。リスニングが難しいと感じる原因の1つでもあります。

✔ **頻出単語チェック！** **Listening Section**

語句と意味を品詞に気をつけながら結びつけてみましょう。

1. musical instrument (   )   a. not interesting
2. favorite (   )   b. to interrupt someone
3. excellent (   )   c. for example, a guitar, a piano or a violin
4. dull [adj.] (   )   d. the people watching a presentation or event
5. taste [n.] (   )   e. a show
6. audience (   )   f. something that someone likes the best
7. disturb (   )   g. liking of particular kinds of things
8. performance (   )   h. very good

Listening Section

PART 1　写真描写問題　🔊 1-15, 16

> *Check Point!*　1人の人物の動作について述べる例を見てみましょう。
> The woman's playing the piano.

それぞれの写真について、4つの説明文の中から最も適切なものを1つずつ選びましょう。

1.

Ⓐ Ⓑ Ⓒ Ⓓ

2.

Ⓐ Ⓑ Ⓒ Ⓓ

PART 2　応答問題　 1-17-21

> *Check Point!*　When の疑問文なら後に続く助動詞の時制に注意しましょう。
> When did you get back from the movie?

それぞれの設問の応答として最も適切なものを1つずつ選びましょう。

3. Mark your answer on your answer sheet.　Ⓐ Ⓑ Ⓒ

4. Mark your answer on your answer sheet.　Ⓐ Ⓑ Ⓒ

5. Mark your answer on your answer sheet.　Ⓐ Ⓑ Ⓒ

6. Mark your answer on your answer sheet.　Ⓐ Ⓑ Ⓒ

7. Mark your answer on your answer sheet.　Ⓐ Ⓑ Ⓒ

> ***Check Point!*** 「会話の主題は何か」 大きく捉えましょう。
> What is the main topic of the conversation?

会話についての設問に対し、最も適切なものを1つずつ選びましょう。

8. What is the main topic of the
conversation?
(A) Their upcoming dinner
(B) The acting in the movie
(C) The movie they just watched
(D) Action movies and love stories

9. How did the man feel about the
movie?
(A) It was very good.
(B) It made him fall asleep.
(C) The acting was excellent.
(D) The action was dull.

10. What does the woman think about
action movies?
(A) She usually finds them dull.
(B) She wants to see one with a
friend.
(C) She likes the actors in the
movies.
(D) She likes them more than love
stories.

> ***Check Point!*** 説明文の 「目的は何か」 大きく捉えましょう。
> What is the purpose of the message?

説明文についての設問に対し、最も適切なものを1つずつ選びましょう。

11. What is the purpose of the
message?
(A) To explain some rules
(B) To describe the 15-minute break
(C) To thank the audience for
attending
(D) To ask people to go to the lobby

12. What will happen after the play?
(A) Coffee and tea will be available.
(B) There will be a 15-minute break.
(C) People can take photos of the
actors.
(D) The audience can eat or drink.

13. What does the speaker ask the
audience to do?
(A) Take photographs during the
play
(B) Finish drinking their tea and
coffee
(C) Keep their mobile phones off
(D) Go on stage with the actors

Grammar Review　不定代名詞

■不定代名詞の one / another / (the) others についてまとめてみます。

人（物）が2人（つ）の場合、一方を one で受けます。残りは1人（つ）と決まっていますので、the other と定冠詞を付けます。3人（つ）の場合は最初を one、次を another とし、最後は残り1人（つ）と決まっていますので the other とします。4人（つ）以上の場合は残りの数に注意します。複数残っているので、the others と複数形にします。

《例題》各空所に入れるべき最も適切な語句を1つ選んで、その記号を書きなさい。

1. There are seven workers from overseas in my office. One is from Taiwan, three are from China, and ------- are from the US.
   (A) another　　(B) other　　(C) the other　　(D) the others

■再帰代名詞のうち1人称 (I, we) と2人称 (you) では所有格の代名詞 +self となります。ただし、3人称 (he, she, it, they) では目的格 +self となることに注意します。

2. Did you enjoy ------- at the party last night?
   (A) you　　(B) your　　(C) yourself　　(D) yours

Reading Section

✔ 頻出単語チェック！　**Reading Section**

単語と意味を品詞に気をつけながら結びつけてみましょう。

1. remove [v.] (　)
2. critic (　)
3. previous (　)
4. science-fiction (　)
5. exciting (　)
6. disappointing (　)
7. favor [n.] (　)
8. entertain (　)

a. a journalist that reviews food or art
b. to do something to help someone have fun
c. a type of story that is often about the future and space
d. making someone feel excited
e. something that you do to help someone
f. to take off
g. the one before this
h. not as good as someone hoped

> **Check Point!** 文法問題：不定代名詞と再帰代名詞、語彙問題：動詞
> 代名詞を選ぶには、もともとの名詞を見極めましょう。

それぞれの空所に入れるのに最も適切なものを1つずつ選びましょう。

14. The movie was reviewed by a dozen newspaper critics, but ------- of them said it was good.
(A) none
(B) neither
(C) nobody
(D) nothing

Ⓐ Ⓑ Ⓒ Ⓓ

15. Parents often take their children to the park when it's sunny, but very ------- take them there on rainy days.
(A) any
(B) few
(C) both
(D) some

Ⓐ Ⓑ Ⓒ Ⓓ

16. All of her friends were busy on Saturday night, so Beth decided to watch a movie by ------- at home.
(A) she
(B) her
(C) hers
(D) herself

Ⓐ Ⓑ Ⓒ Ⓓ

17. One of the world's most famous classical pianists will ------- at the concert.
(A) deliver
(B) expand
(C) perform
(D) remember

Ⓐ Ⓑ Ⓒ Ⓓ

18. The number of people ------- the play tonight was much larger than on the previous night.
(A) passing
(B) believing
(C) attending
(D) removing

Ⓐ Ⓑ Ⓒ Ⓓ

PART 6   長文穴埋め問題

Check Point!   語彙問題：形容詞
文章挿入問題：空所が文中なら前後と矛盾のない文を選びましょう。

それぞれの空所に入れるのに最も適切なものを1つずつ選びましょう。

Glory Riders is a very interesting science-fiction movie. It is ------- 200 years in
19.
the future. The world is very different. The weather is much hotter and most of
the world is a desert. The design is fantastic with lots of amazing buildings and
costumes. Unfortunately, the performance of lead actor Gregory Taylor was
------- . He's usually a very good actor, who plays interesting characters. ------- .
20.   **21.**
They, along with the exciting story, mean that this is definitely worth watching.

19. (A) set
    (B) sets
    (C) setting
    (D) to be setting

20. (A) changing
    (B) improving
    (C) disappointing
    (D) moving

21. (A) His many fans will probably not mind.
    (B) And the same is true in this movie.
    (C) But in *Glory Riders*, his character is boring.
    (D) The other actors, however, are really good.

Check Point!　E-mail（1つの文書）
差出人と受信者との関係やメールの目的を読み取りましょう。

文章を読んで、それぞれの設問の答えとして最も適切なものを1つずつ選びましょう。

✉ E-MAIL

To:	Ann Williams <a-williams@eznet.com>
From:	Joe Andrews <jandrews@legal-partners.com>
Date:	September 30
Subject:	A good musical?

Hi Ann,

Could you do me a favor? Next week a client of mine is visiting from Tokyo. I'm supposed to entertain him during his stay here in New York.

I plan to take him to dinner, but I thought he might enjoy a Broadway musical, too. His English is good, so he won't have any problem understanding it. But I'm not sure what musical would be the best. Since you often go to the theater, I thought you might be able to recommend something good.

My client is around 30. He has a great sense of humor, so maybe we should choose a funny musical. Anyway, if you could give me some suggestions, I'd really appreciate it.

Thanks!

Joe

---

22. For whom is the e-mail intended?
(A) A friend
(B) A musical star
(C) A client
(D) A Broadway actress

23. What did Joe say about the client?
(A) He is a fan of Broadway musicals.
(B) He's staying for a week.
(C) He's lived in New York for 30 years.
(D) He might prefer to watch a comedy.

Business

:: *Warm up* Dictation Practice   1-26

各空所に入る語（1以外は短縮形）を、音声を聞いて書き入れてみましょう。

1. I (   ) lend you my PC.
2. I (   ) lend you my PC.
3. (   ) your boss?
4. (   ) going to visit the British company.
5. (   ) been in France for six months.
6. (   ) never been to a foreign country on business before.
7. (   ) visit the client to sell their product.
8. He (   ) complete the sales report by noon.
9. She (   ) be at the meeting because she has a headache.
10. (   ) the difference between the two products?

🔍 Points to Dictate

助動詞や疑問詞、be 動詞などを含む短縮形の聞き取りです。She has と She is の短縮形＝ She's のように形が同じものがあります。また、can と can't のように 180 度意味が異なる短縮形にも要注意です。自分でも言えるように練習しましょう。

✔ 頻出単語チェック！ Listening Section

語句と意味を品詞に気をつけながら結びつけてみましょう。

1. issue [n.] (   )
2. hand out (   )
3. product (   )
4. increase [v.] (   )
5. afford (   )
6. release [v.] (   )
7. press conference (   )
8. manufacturer (   )

a. a topic or problem
b. a meeting where someone answers questions from journalists
c. to give something to people
d. a thing that companies make and sell
e. to have enough money for something
f. a company that makes things
g. to make something become bigger
h. to make a product available to buy

PART 1 写真描写問題 1-27, 28

Check Point! 複数のうちの1人の動作について述べる例を見てみましょう。
A man is pointing to some memos.

それぞれの写真について、4つの説明文の中から最も適切なものを1つずつ選びましょう。

1.

Ⓐ Ⓑ Ⓒ Ⓓ

2.

Ⓐ Ⓑ Ⓒ Ⓓ

PART 2 応答問題 1-29-33

Check Point! Where の疑問文なら in, at, to を伴う「場所」を連想しましょう。
Where did you get your hair cut?

それぞれの設問の応答として最も適切なものを1つずつ選びましょう。

3. Mark your answer on your answer sheet.　　Ⓐ Ⓑ Ⓒ

4. Mark your answer on your answer sheet.　　Ⓐ Ⓑ Ⓒ

5. Mark your answer on your answer sheet.　　Ⓐ Ⓑ Ⓒ

6. Mark your answer on your answer sheet.　　Ⓐ Ⓑ Ⓒ

7. Mark your answer on your answer sheet.　　Ⓐ Ⓑ Ⓒ

PART 3   会話問題   1-34, 35

> *Check Point!*   2人が「何について話しているのか」大きく捉えましょう。
> What are the speakers discussing?

会話についての設問に対し、最も適切なものを1つずつ選びましょう。

8. What are the speakers discussing?
(A) The clothes for this year
(B) The prices of new products
(C) The best way to increase sales
(D) The TV commercial they made

9. What does the woman suggest?
(A) Creating a sales goal
(B) Assisting more customers
(C) Making a new TV commercial
(D) Lowering costs for commercials

10. What is the man concerned about?
(A) The woman's idea may be too expensive.
(B) The TV commercial may look cheap.
(C) A ten percent sales increase will not be enough.
(D) The store cannot afford to stay in business.

PART 4   説明文問題   1-36, 37

> *Check Point!*   「何が発表されているのか」大きく捉えましょう。
> What is being announced?

説明文についての設問に対し、最も適切なものを1つずつ選びましょう。

11. What is being announced?
(A) The release of some new products
(B) A special sale at computer stores
(C) A problem with a battery product
(D) A five percent discount on all electronics products

12. What does the speaker ask the listeners to do?
(A) Visit an electronics store
(B) Attend a press conference
(C) Check out some information online
(D) Get a new battery for their computers

13. Where does the speaker most likely work?
(A) An electronics store
(B) A magazine company
(C) A computer company
(D) A battery manufacturer

Part 5 形式の問題を通して見出しの文法項目をチェックします。

■現在時制で注意が必要なことは、「現在の状態」「習慣」「物の性質」「変わることのない真理」「近い未来」の5つの用法です。いずれも現在時制が使われます。

《例題》各空所に入れるべき最も適切な語句を1つ選んで、その記号を書きなさい。

1. We usually ------- that brand available.
   (A) has had　　(B) have been having　　(C) have　　(D) are having

2. The last train for Chicago ------- at 11 P.M.
   (A) leaving　　(B) is left　　(C) leaves　　(D) will be left

■過去時制は、話をしている瞬間より以前に起こったり、存在した事柄を表します。事柄の起こった時点で動作が終了しているかどうかを見極めます。

3. Jack skipped lunch because ------- so much work to do.
   (A) there are　　(B) there was　　(C) he has been　　(D) he can have

Reading Section

✔ 頻出単語チェック！ Reading Section

単語と意味を品詞に気をつけながら結びつけてみましょう。

1. profit [n.] (　　)
2. compete (　　)
3. funds (　　)
4. invest (　　)
5. emerging (　　)
6. expansion (　　)
7. submit (　　)
8. ensure (　　)

a. the money that you get from selling something minus the costs
b. money
c. to make sure
d. the increase in size or number of something
e. to give money to a company because you hope to get more back in the future
f. to try to do better than others
g. new
h. to formally send something

PART 5　短文穴埋め問題

Check Point!　文法問題：現在・過去の時制、語彙問題：動詞
時制を決定づける語句に注目しましょう。

それぞれの空所に入れるのに最も適切なものを 1 つずつ選びましょう。

14. Japanese automakers ------- a lot of cars to the United States.
    (A) export
    (B) exports
    (C) exporting
    (D) is exported　Ⓐ Ⓑ Ⓒ Ⓓ

15. The meeting went well, so the trip to London ------- a big success.
    (A) is
    (B) was
    (C) were
    (D) are　Ⓐ Ⓑ Ⓒ Ⓓ

16. The company often ------- business in China, but it's hard to make a profit.
    (A) did
    (B) does
    (C) was doing
    (D) doing　Ⓐ Ⓑ Ⓒ Ⓓ

17. Electronics companies won't be able to ------- in the global market unless they can reduce their costs.
    (A) divide
    (B) believe
    (C) compete
    (D) examine　Ⓐ Ⓑ Ⓒ Ⓓ

18. Every Monday, the company ------- a meeting to discuss sales results of the previous week.
    (A) stays
    (B) holds
    (C) breaks
    (D) frames　Ⓐ Ⓑ Ⓒ Ⓓ

> ***Check Point!***　語彙問題：動詞
> 文章挿入問題：空所が文中なら前後と矛盾のない文を選びましょう。

それぞれの空所に入れるのに最も適切なものを１つずつ選びましょう。

This Year's Business Results

We are happy to report that last year we earned very high profits as a result of increased sales. ---**19.**---. In particular, our sales in Europe were excellent thanks to the expansion of our production facilities there. This success came with challenges, though. There are several issues that we ---**20.**--- throughout the year, including the corporate tax increases in some countries. Another problem was the difficulty in finding enough high-quality workers in some regions of the world. But we have been working hard to ---**21.**--- these issues, and our outlook for the future is positive.

---

19. (A) For this reason, we are looking to enter some overseas markets.
　　(B) In fact, our sales for the year were 32 percent higher than in the previous year.
　　(C) You will notice that our latest product is quite promising.
　　(D) These extra funds will be used to invest in emerging markets.

20. (A) face
　　(B) faced
　　(C) are facing
　　(D) will face

21. (A) address
　　(B) measure
　　(C) challenge
　　(D) prove

PART 7   読解問題

Check Point!   メモ（1つの文書）
何のために、誰が書いたメモなのかを探りながら読みましょう。

文章を読んで、それぞれの設問の答えとして最も適切なものを1つずつ選びましょう。

MEMO

This is a reminder to all employees planning to take a week or more of vacation during the summer. If possible, applications should be submitted before the end of May. We ask for this to be done to ensure that there is an adequate number of staff at any given time during the summer. Last summer, as you know, too many employees in the Sales Department took their vacation in mid-July, which resulted in some problems.

Those employees who submit their applications for vacation the earliest will be given top priority. So please try to finalize your summer plans soon. The application forms are available from the Human Resources Department.

Thank you for your understanding.

---

22. What is the purpose of this memo?

(A) To encourage employees to not take vacation

(B) To tell employees the May schedule

(C) To ask employees to apply for vacation

(D) To introduce the Human Resources Department

23. What happened last summer?

(A) A lot of employees took a vacation at the same time.

(B) The company had problems throughout July.

(C) Employees took a summer trip together in mid-July.

(D) Sales Department employees forgot to fill out their applications.

The Office

:: *Warm up* — **Dictation Practice** 1-38

それぞれの空所に入る語を、音声を聞いて書き入れてみましょう。

1. I (   ) (   ) advice.

2. He (   ) (   ) advice.

3. I will (   ) (   ) at the conference room.

4. I (   ) (   ) to tell me how to use the new copier.

5. The manager (   ) (   ) to visit his office.

6. (   ) (   ) mind my opening the window?

7. (   ) (   ) attend Kim's party last night?

8. Our investment will increase by eight percent (   ) (   ).

9. She (   ) (   ) make a presentation tomorrow.

10. Our boss (   ) (   ) comments on our report.

🔍 Points to Dictate

品詞に関係なく２つの語が連続して１語のように聞こえるケースの練習です。ここで最も大切なのは、三単現や複数形の -s、さらに過去形の -ed などの音を前後関係を考え正確に聞き取れるようになることです。

☑ 頻出単語チェック！ | **Listening Section**

語句と意味を品詞に気をつけながら結びつけてみましょう。

1. put away (   )   **a.** to go to a meeting or event

2. unplug (   )   **b.** a formal business meeting

3. overtime [n.] (   )   **c.** to tidy or store something

4. attend (   )   **d.** to disconnect an appliance (from the power or from another device)

5. conference (   )

6. come up with (   )   **e.** things needed for work in an office (for example, pens)

7. office supplies (   )

8. hook up (   )   **f.** extra working time after the usual finish time

    g. to think of or create something

    h. to connect something (to another thing or to the Internet)

Listening Section

PART 1   写真描写問題

1-39, 40

Check Point!

複数のうちの１人の動作について述べる例を見てみましょう。
A woman is putting away her tablet.

それぞれの写真について、４つの説明文の中から最も適切なものを１つずつ選びましょう。

1.

Ⓐ Ⓑ Ⓒ Ⓓ

2.

Ⓐ Ⓑ Ⓒ Ⓓ

PART 2   応答問題

1-41-45

Check Point!

Who の疑問文では人名、肩書き、部署名を連想しましょう。
Who left this memo on my desk?

それぞれの設問の応答として最も適切なものを１つずつ選びましょう。

3. Mark your answer on your answer sheet.　　　Ⓐ Ⓑ Ⓒ

4. Mark your answer on your answer sheet.　　　Ⓐ Ⓑ Ⓒ

5. Mark your answer on your answer sheet.　　　Ⓐ Ⓑ Ⓒ

6. Mark your answer on your answer sheet.　　　Ⓐ Ⓑ Ⓒ

7. Mark your answer on your answer sheet.　　　Ⓐ Ⓑ Ⓒ

Check Point! 「会話の目的は何か」を全体から聞き取りましょう。
What is the purpose of the conversation?

会話についての設問に対し、最も適切なものを1つずつ選びましょう。

8. What is the purpose of the conversation?
   (A) To interview a person for a new job
   (B) To explain the computer to a worker
   (C) To come up with a new office system
   (D) To show a new employee her work space

9. What will the man do next?
   (A) Introduce the woman's coworkers
   (B) Explain the computer system
   (C) Show the woman the office supplies
   (D) Hook up more of the computers

10. What does the woman want to do now?
    (A) Listen to the man's ideas
    (B) Find out about her coworkers
    (C) Ask the man some questions
    (D) Learn more about her computer

PART 4　説明文問題 1-48, 49

Check Point! 「メッセージの目的は何か」大きく捉えましょう。
What is the purpose of the announcement?

説明文についての設問に対し、最も適切なものを1つずつ選びましょう。

11. What is the purpose of the announcement?
    (A) To explain her old career
    (B) To discuss the afternoon meeting
    (C) To introduce herself to colleagues
    (D) To talk about the Sales Department

12. What will the woman do today?
    (A) Create a new sales strategy
    (B) Start working as a sales manager
    (C) Move her desk near the window
    (D) Move to the Food Department

13. What will happen this afternoon?
    (A) The woman will introduce herself.
    (B) A sales strategy meeting will be held.
    (C) A new sales manager will be chosen.
    (D) Sue Fields will arrive.

Grammar Review　現在完了

■現在完了は文字通り「現在＋完了形」で、時の視点は話をしている「現在」にあります。過去に起こった事柄を現在の視点から見て、「完了・結果・経験・継続」などの働きを通じて現在に結びつけるときに使われます。「完了・結果」によく出てくる副詞は just, already, yet。「経験」では before, once, twice, three times, ever, never、「継続」では for, since がよく使われます。

《例題》各空所に入れるべき最も適切な語句を 1 つ選んで、その記号を書きなさい。

1. Bill Aniston ------- living in Paris for two years now.
   (A) is　　(B) was　　(C) has been　　(D) had been

2. Janet ------- the client's office in New York twice.
   (A) are visiting　　(B) are visited　　(C) has been visiting
   (D) has visited

3. Alice, ------- writing your sales report yet?
   (A) are you finish　　(B) are you finishing　　(C) do you finish
   (D) have you finished

Reading Section

✔ 頻出単語チェック！　Reading Section

語句と意味を品詞に気をつけながら結びつけてみましょう。

1. CEO (　　)
2. partner (　　)
3. fix [v.] (　　)
4. wonder [v.] (　　)
5. reschedule (　　)
6. bother [v.] (　　)
7. go off (　　)
8. disable (　　)

a. to change the day and time for a planned meeting or event
b. Chief Executive Officer; the leader of a company
c. a company that works closely with another
d. to switch it off
e. to repair something
f. to make a loud noise
g. to disturb
h. to think

> *Check Point!*　文法問題：現在完了、語彙問題：名詞
> 時・期間を表す語句を伴って完了形を作ることに注目しましょう。

それぞれの空所に入れるのに最も適切なものを１つずつ選びましょう。

14. Brad and Megan ------- in the same office for 15 years, but only one of them will become the new manager.
(A) have been work
(B) have been working
(C) have been worked
(D) had been working
Ⓐ Ⓑ Ⓒ Ⓓ

15. The CEO ------- our partners in Belgium five times so far this year.
(A) visits
(B) is visiting
(C) has visited
(D) had visited
Ⓐ Ⓑ Ⓒ Ⓓ

16. The copy machine -------, so we need to ask somebody to come and fix it.
(A) is breaking
(B) breaks
(C) has broken
(D) was breaking
Ⓐ Ⓑ Ⓒ Ⓓ

17. The company had to move to a much bigger office after it doubled the number of its -------.
(A) losses
(B) fixtures
(C) reminders
(D) employees
Ⓐ Ⓑ Ⓒ Ⓓ

18. The ------- of our office, right next to the train station, is very convenient.
(A) price
(B) height
(C) location
(D) scenery
Ⓐ Ⓑ Ⓒ Ⓓ

PART 6　長文穴埋め問題

それぞれの空所に入れるのに最も適切なものを 1 つずつ選びましょう。

✉ E-MAIL

To:	Jill Davies <davies@gdr-corp.com>
From:	Paul Madison <paulmad@tripedmail.com>
Date:	June 10
Subject:	Running late

Hi Jill,

I'm still on the train. It looks like I won't arrive at the office for at least another 45 minutes or so.

Could you let Mr. Peters know that I'm going to be late? -------. **19.** If he's free at 2 o'clock I could meet him then. -------, **20.** we'll have to reschedule for another day.

Also, I was wondering if you're free for lunch today. I'd like to hear more about some of the ideas you have for new product designs. If lunch ------- **21.** good, I can meet you around 12:30 just outside the entrance to the building.

Regards,

Paul

19. (A) I was supposed to have a meeting with him this morning.
    (B) I want to schedule a meeting with him today.
    (C) He may have forgotten about our meeting today.
    (D) We're meeting with some clients later.

20. (A) Likewise
    (B) Naturally
    (C) Otherwise
    (D) Generally

21. (A) sounds
    (B) sounded
    (C) is sounding
    (D) has sounded

文章を読んで、それぞれの設問の答えとして最も適切なものを１つずつ選びましょう。

Ken Lee   **7:49 A.M.**
Hi, Helen. I'm really sorry to bother you so early on your day off, but I was hoping you could help me with something.

Helen Quinn   **7:50 A.M.**
Sure. What's the matter?

Ken Lee   **7:51 A.M.**
I'm the first person at the office today, and I'm not sure how to open the door without the alarm going off. Usually, there's someone here before me.

Helen Quinn   **7:52 A.M.**
You have a key, right? So use that to open the door at the back of the building on the ground floor. When you walk inside, there'll be a keypad on your left. Enter the code #8731 to disable the alarm.

Ken Lee   **7:53 A.M.**
Thank you. I think I understand.

Helen Quinn   **7:53 A.M.**
I can call you and walk you through it if you want.

Ken Lee   **7:54 A.M.**
That's OK. I'll manage. Thank you, again. And sorry for bothering you.

---

22. What is indicated about Ms. Quinn?
(A) She is the office manager.
(B) She is always the first person at the office.
(C) She has a different schedule than Mr. Lee.
(D) She is a new employee.

23. At 7:54 A.M., what does Mr. Lee mean when he writes, "I'll manage"?
(A) He will ask someone else to do it.
(B) He will get help opening the door.
(C) He is confident that he can perform the task.
(D) He is accessing the security system.

Telephone

Warm up   Dictation Practice   1-50

それぞれの空所に入る語を、音声を聞いて書き入れてみましょう。

1. He called his tennis (   ) (   ) he left his wallet there.
2. She quit her telephone company (   ) (   ) can't find a new one.
3. Please call me in the morning if you (   ) (   ) talk to me.
4. My brand new smartphone is fantastic; it's (   ) (   ).
5. There's a public phone right (   ) (   ) our building.
6. He had to (   ) (   ) of the company telephone system.
7. Will you (   ) (   ) with my smartphone?
8. Mary called the college to ask details of the (   ) (   ).
9. I think now is the (   ) (   ) to switch to a new phone.
10. She was drinking (   ) (   ) when she received a call from her friend.

Points to Dictate

前の単語の最後の音と、次の単語の最初の音が同じ場合に、一方の音が脱落してしまうケースを練習しましょう。例えば、stop paying(p+p) は≒ stopaying のように、hot topic(t+t) は≒ hotopic のように聞こえます。

✔ 頻出単語チェック！   Listening Section

語句と意味を品詞に気をつけながら結びつけてみましょう。

1. bill [n.] (   )
2. look up (   )
3. offer [v.] (   )
4. temporary (   )
5. remodeling (   )
6. go out of business (   )
7. appreciation (   )
8. patience (   )

a. to find information in a book or on the Internet
b. to say you can do something to help someone
c. changing something to a new style
d. a notice of how much money someone must pay for something
e. to close a company because it is not making enough money
f. waiting without becoming angry
g. showing that someone values something that a person did
h. for a short-time; not for ever

PART 1　写真描写問題　　　　　　　　　　　　　 1-51, 52

> *Check Point!* ＼ 人物の動作について述べる例を見てみましょう。
> He's reading a message on his computer.

それぞれの写真について、4つの説明文の中から最も適切なものを1つずつ選びましょう。

1.

Ⓐ Ⓑ Ⓒ Ⓓ

2.

Ⓐ Ⓑ Ⓒ Ⓓ

PART 2　応答問題　　　　　　　　　　　　　　 1-53-57

> *Check Point!* ＼ Why の疑問文では理由を述べている文章を探しましょう。
> Why is all the office furniture covered?

それぞれの設問の応答として最も適切なものを1つずつ選びましょう。

3. Mark your answer on your answer sheet.　　　　　　Ⓐ Ⓑ Ⓒ

4. Mark your answer on your answer sheet.　　　　　　Ⓐ Ⓑ Ⓒ

5. Mark your answer on your answer sheet.　　　　　　Ⓐ Ⓑ Ⓒ

6. Mark your answer on your answer sheet.　　　　　　Ⓐ Ⓑ Ⓒ

7. Mark your answer on your answer sheet.　　　　　　Ⓐ Ⓑ Ⓒ

PART 3 会話問題   1-58, 59

> ***Check Point!*** 「話し手の一方が何を提案しているのか」聞き取りましょう。
> What does the woman suggest the man do?

会話についての設問に対し、最も適切なものを1つずつ選びましょう。

8. What does the woman suggest the man do?
   (A) Call her on his phone
   (B) Use his mobile phone today
   (C) Buy a new mobile phone
   (D) Check the Internet now

9. What does the man say about his phone?
   (A) It is too old.
   (B) It suits his needs.
   (C) It is very convenient.
   (D) It is time to buy a new one.

10. What does the woman offer to do?
    (A) Help the man buy a phone
    (B) Pay for the man's new phone
    (C) Let the man use her phone
    (D) Check some Web sites for the man

PART 4 説明文問題   1-60, 61

> ***Check Point!*** 「メッセージの主題は何か」大きく捉えましょう。
> What is the subject of the announcement?

説明文についての設問に対し、最も適切なものを1つずつ選びましょう。

11. What is the subject of the announcement?
    (A) The temporary closing of a restaurant
    (B) The opening of a pizza restaurant
    (C) A special offer for today only
    (D) A restaurant going out of business

12. What will happen on March 1?
    (A) The restaurant will reopen.
    (B) Tony's Pizza Parlor will close.
    (C) All food at the restaurant will be on sale.
    (D) The restaurant will close for remodeling.

13. What will customers be able to do next month?
    (A) Visit another restaurant
    (B) Order take-out for the first time
    (C) Get a free pizza
    (D) Sit outside the restaurant

Grammar Review 前置詞 [時・期間]

■前置詞も頻繁に出題されています。今回は「時」を示す前置詞にフォーカスします。
   ① 年月・日時を示す：**at** seven o'clock, **on** Mondays, **in** 1994
   ② 時の起点を示す：**from** 9:00, **since** last night, **after** my birthday
   ③ 時の終点を示す：**till** 6 o'clock, **until** 12:00, **by** noon, **before** Christmas
   ④ 時の経過を示す：**in** ten minutes, **within** two days, **after** three weeks

《例題》各空所に入れるべき最も適切な語句を1つ選んで、その記号を書きなさい。

   1. The item you ordered is not available at this time. Please reorder ------- a few weeks.
   (A) in   (B) for   (C) until   (D) from

■「期間」を示す前置詞には **for** a few minutes, **during** the summer, **through** the winter があります。for は後ろに three weeks のような数詞の付いた語句を伴います。
   during はある特定の期間を示し、through はある期間全部を通して継続することを示します。

   2. The game of bowling has been played ------- 7,000 years.
   (A) since   (B) although   (C) for more than   (D) until the next

Reading Section

✓ 頻出単語チェック！ Reading Section

単語と意味を品詞に気をつけながら結びつけてみましょう。

1. call [n.] (   )
2. line [n.] (   )
3. value [v.] (   )
4. strive (   )
5. variety (   )
6. available (   )
7. procedure (   )
8. contact [v.] (   )

a. to respect and think highly of
b. a number of different types
c. communications by telephone
d. a part of the telephone network
e. to communicate with someone by phone, e-mail or letter, etc.
f. not busy; free
g. to work hard to achieve something
h. an official way of doing something

PART 5　短文穴埋め問題

　文法問題：前置詞（時・期間）、語彙問題：名詞
時・期間を示す前置詞はどのような語句と共に使われるかを覚えましょう。

それぞれの空所に入れるのに最も適切なものを1つずつ選びましょう。

14. Mr. Stevens waited ------- 9 P.M. for a phone call from his client, but it never
came.
(A) until
(B) during
(C) within
(D) between　　　Ⓐ Ⓑ Ⓒ Ⓓ

15. The customer service department receives most of its calls ------- the afternoon,
from around 2 P.M. to 4 P.M.
(A) at
(B) in
(C) on
(D) by　　　Ⓐ Ⓑ Ⓒ Ⓓ

16. Today, Ms. Jackson was on the phone ------- over an hour to explain something
to a customer.
(A) by
(B) for
(C) till
(D) from　　　Ⓐ Ⓑ Ⓒ Ⓓ

17. James had to leave a ------- on Sue's phone because she wasn't home.
(A) call
(B) note
(C) memo
(D) message　　　Ⓐ Ⓑ Ⓒ Ⓓ

18. I've called this number half a dozen times, but each time the ------- was busy.
(A) line
(B) dial
(C) street
(D) call　　　Ⓐ Ⓑ Ⓒ Ⓓ

> *Check Point!*　語彙問題：動詞
> 文章挿入問題：空所が文末なら文章の結びとなる文を選びましょう。

それぞれの空所に入れるのに最も適切なものを1つずつ選びましょう。

Customer Service Line

At Stevens Electronics, we --------- our customers, and we strive to bring you the
19.
best service possible. For this reason, we have a variety of options for
contacting our customer service team.

For urgent requests, you can call us on 802-123-4567. Phone operators are
available from 8 A.M. to 6:30 P.M., Monday to Friday, or from 9 A.M. to 5 P.M. on
Saturday and Sunday. For all other issues, please e-mail us at this address:
support@stevenselectronics.com. --------- that a response may take up to three
20.
business days.

Finally, there is also the option of visiting one of our stores in person. We have
over 650 stores throughout the country. Stop by to speak with our highly-
trained, friendly staff about technical issues, order questions, or any other
concerns you may have. ---------.
21.

---

19. (A) contact
　　 (B) assess
　　 (C) value
　　 (D) dedicate

20. (A) Note
　　 (B) Notes
　　 (C) Noted
　　 (D) Noting

21. (A) All requests must be made directly to our home office.
　　 (B) Let us explain the contact procedures.
　　 (C) We hope that you will consider joining our team.
　　 (D) We thank you for your continued support.

PART 7　読解問題

Check Point!　お知らせ（1つの文書）
何のお知らせか、誰が書いたものかを探りながら読みましょう。

文章を読んで、それぞれの設問の答えとして最も適切なものを1つずつ選びましょう。

X987 Phones

Please note that we have completely sold out of the new X987 mobile phones. We have ordered some new stock, but it will be at least two weeks before they arrive – and we have been told that we will only be able to get the black and white models in this first shipment. Other colors are unlikely to be available for at least a month. So, if you are interested in buying one of these phones, please talk to a member of staff and we will add your name to the waiting list. Thank you for your understanding.

22. What is the purpose of the notice?
(A) To tell people how to sell their phones
(B) To introduce some new colors for a product
(C) To explain how to order a popular product
(D) To confirm that a new product is now available

23. What is mentioned about the phone?
(A) It is not working correctly.
(B) It is selling fast – except the black and white models.
(C) It takes a long time for staff to set up.
(D) It is available in several colors.

UNIT 6

Letters & E-mails

Warm up | **Dictation Practice** 1-62

それぞれの空所に入る語を、音声を聞いて書き入れてみましょう。

1. Can I send a letter from (　　　　　) (　　　　　)?
2. I need to buy some stamps at (　　　　　) (　　　　　).
3. He sent a couple of e-mail messages while eating a (　　　　　)
   (　　　　　).
4. I couldn't respond to his e-mail until the (　　　　　) (　　　　　).
5. She (　　　　　) (　　　　　) in her chair and started writing an e-mail.
6. He mentioned in his letter that he had a (　　　　　) (　　　　　) last year.
7. He sat at the (　　　　　) (　　　　　) to read an e-mail message.
8. The (　　　　　) (　　　　　) was too small for her to write a letter.
9. She said it was a (　　　　　) (　　　　　) today.
10. This is a (　　　　　) (　　　　　) on how to write a letter.

> 🔍 **Points to Dictate**
>
> 前の単語の最後の音と、次の単語の最初の音が似た音の場合にも一方の音が脱落して聞こえるケースがあります。後ろの単語の最初の音が残ります。例えば、gapbetween(p+b) は ≒ gabetween のように聞こえます。

☑ 頻出単語チェック! **Listening Section**

語句と意味を品詞に気をつけながら結びつけてみましょう。

1. deliver (　　)
2. attach (　　)
3. text message (　　)
4. get in touch (　　)
5. respond (　　)
6. time difference (　　)
7. handout (　　)
8. expert [n.] (　　)

a. to reply to someone
b. a document that is given to people at a meeting or presentation
c. to take something to a particular place
d. a short message sent from phone to phone
e. the difference in time in different countries
f. someone who knows a lot about a particular topic
g. to communicate with someone
h. to include a file with an e-mail

Listening Section

PART 1 写真描写問題 1-63, 64

> *Check Point!* 人物と対象となる物について述べる例を見てみましょう。
> He's holding some pens.

それぞれの写真について、4つの説明文の中から最も適切なものを1つずつ選びましょう。

1.

Ⓐ Ⓑ Ⓒ Ⓓ

2.

Ⓐ Ⓑ Ⓒ Ⓓ

PART 2 応答問題 1-65-69

> *Check Point!* How+ 助動詞で「方法」が問われている例を見てみましょう。
> How should I send you the package?

それぞれの設問の応答として最も適切なものを1つずつ選びましょう。

3. Mark your answer on your answer sheet. Ⓐ Ⓑ Ⓒ

4. Mark your answer on your answer sheet. Ⓐ Ⓑ Ⓒ

5. Mark your answer on your answer sheet. Ⓐ Ⓑ Ⓒ

6. Mark your answer on your answer sheet. Ⓐ Ⓑ Ⓒ

7. Mark your answer on your answer sheet. Ⓐ Ⓑ Ⓒ

> *Check Point!* 「話者が何をしているのか」聞き取りましょう。
> What is the woman doing?

会話についての設問に対し、最も適切なものを１つずつ選びましょう。

8. What is the woman doing?
   (A) Contacting the man
   (B) Writing an e-mail
   (C) Visiting New York
   (D) Preparing for a trip

9. What does the woman say about
   her trip to Paris?
   (A) It is a personal trip.
   (B) It takes six hours to get there.
   (C) It is free.
   (D) It is a business trip.

10. What is the man concerned about?
    (A) Her contact details
    (B) Her return date
    (C) Her schedule
    (D) Her hotel

PART 4 説明文問題 1-72, 73

> *Check Point!* 「話し手は誰か」を問う形を知っておきましょう。
> Who is the speaker?

説明文についての設問に対し、最も適切なものを１つずつ選びましょう。

11. Who is the speaker?
    (A) Mr. Jeffers
    (B) A new employee
    (C) A company client
    (D) A computer expert

12. What are the listeners asked to do?
    (A) Use the company e-mail for work
    (B) Hook up their own computers
    (C) Contact Mr. Jeffers
    (D) Check their e-mails

13. What will happen later?
    (A) Mr. Jeffers will provide some
        information.
    (B) Mr. Jeffers will hook up the
        computers.
    (C) Employees will be able to use
        their private e-mail.
    (D) The e-mail addresses will be
        handed out.

Grammar Review   前置詞［位置・場所］

■前回に続いて「位置・場所」を示す前置詞を見ていきます。

① at と in：**at** a hotel **in** Boston のように at は比較的狭い地域、in は広い地域に用いる。

②上・下関係を示す：on, over, under など、それぞれの後に the table を補って考える。

③間の位置を示す：**between** the two places（2つの間）、**among** the trees（3つ以上の間）

④運動の方向を示す：walked **along** the road（道に沿って歩いて行った）、walked **across** the road（道を横切って行った）、walked **around** the corner（角を曲がって歩いて行った）

《例題》各空所に入れるべき最も適切な語を1つ選んで、その記号を書きなさい。

1. All of us met ------- the airport lobby at one o'clock.
   (A) by   (B) from   (C) of   (D) at

2. The largest meeting room is ------- the third floor of our main office building.
   (A) on   (B) to   (C) by   (D) from

Reading Section

☑ **頻出単語チェック！**   **Reading Section**

語句と意味を品詞に気をつけながら結びつけてみましょう。

1. receive (   )   **a.** an answer
2. reply [n.] (   )   **b.** to get something from someone
3. competitive (   )   **c.** to be able to use something
4. according to (   )   **d.** a new window that appears automatically on the
5. optimistic (   )   screen
6. furthermore (   )   **e.** wants to win
7. pop-up [n.] (   )   **f.** in the opinion of
8. access [v.] (   )   **g.** also
                          h. feeling positive about something good happening

> **Check Point!**　文法問題：前置詞（位置・場所）、語彙問題：名詞
> 位置・場所を示す前置詞はどのような語句と使われるかを覚え
> ましょう。

それぞれの空所に入れるのに最も適切なものを1つずつ選びましょう。

14. Matthew left some letters ------- the table for Valerie to mail.
(A) on
(B) by
(C) of
(D) at
Ⓐ Ⓑ Ⓒ Ⓓ

15. I was going to be late for the meeting so I wrote a text message to my boss while I was walking ------- the street.
(A) among
(B) between
(C) under
(D) along
Ⓐ Ⓑ Ⓒ Ⓓ

16. Meagan just sent me an e-mail about the party from her new office ------- New York.
(A) on
(B) at
(C) in
(D) by

17. Diane is worried because she has received no ------- to the e-mail she wrote her brother last week.
(A) reply
(B) copy
(C) noise
(D) address
Ⓐ Ⓑ Ⓒ Ⓓ

18. I couldn't find any ------- at the office that were big enough for this document.
(A) mail
(B) reasons
(C) deliveries
(D) envelopes
Ⓐ Ⓑ Ⓒ Ⓓ

PART 6　長文穴埋め問題

それぞれの空所に入れるのに最も適切なものを１つずつ選びましょう。

Dear Professor Naismith,

I hope that you are enjoying the winter holiday.

I am writing to thank you for taking the time to write me a letter of ------- for my
19.
graduate school application. I mailed all of the application forms just before
leaving for my trip to New York City. According to the university, I will find out if I
have been ------- in March.
20.

The graduate program is very competitive so it will be hard to get in. -------. And
21.
even if I am rejected, I think that I will be able to find a good job at an IT
company.

Thanks again for your help!

Sincerely,

Todd Franks

---

19. (A) refusal
(B) reaction
(C) responsibility
(D) recommendation

20. (A) accept
(B) accepted
(C) accepting
(D) acceptable

21. (A) Still, I am very optimistic about
my chances.
(B) However, I don't know what to
do about my application.
(C) Additionally, this is my second
time applying.
(D) Furthermore, your advice was
so helpful.

Check Point! ＼ 広告（1つの文書）
何の広告か、広告主は誰なのかを探りながら読みましょう。

文章を読んで、それぞれの設問の答えとして最も適切なものを1つずつ選びましょう。

Why not try *EZ-CONNECT* ?

It's free!

☑ Do you want to protect your online privacy?
☑ Are you tired of pop-up advertisements?

EZ-CONNECT is a free e-mail service that protects your private information. We never sell information to online advertisers, so you can be confident about your online privacy.

But that's not all: *EZ-CONNECT* is also simple to use. It only takes a few minutes to create your *EZ-CONNECT* e-mail account. You can access your e-mail through our Web site or through our app. Plus, there is no limit on the amount of memory for your account. So why not sign up for *EZ-CONNECT* today? Visit *ez-connect.com* for more information.

---

22. What is being advertised?

(A) An online privacy company

(B) A free e-mail service

(C) A new Web site

(D) An online advertiser

23. What does EZ-connect promise NOT to do?

(A) Charge for extra memory

(B) Change your privacy settings

(C) Sell information to advertisers

(D) Create an app

Health

Dictation Practice 1-74

それぞれの空所に入る語を、音声を聞いて書き入れてみましょう。

1. It's a ( ) ( ) to ask her about healthy food for athletes.
2. The doctor said, "I'm sorry to have ( ) ( ) waiting so long."
3. I ( ) ( ) is necessary for all of us to have a health check.
4. ( ) ( ) call the hospital to make an appointment?
5. It's almost impossible to ( ) ( ) healthy.
6. The view from the ( ) ( ) the mountain made me feel refreshed.
7. I try to exercise every morning by jogging or lifting weights, ( ) ( ).
8. I would like to join a sports gym ( ) ( ).
9. The old city hospital was ( ) ( ) last year for remodeling.
10. There was no medicine left ( ) ( ) in the first-aid box.

🔍 **Points to Dictate**

前の語の最後の音が次の語の最初の音と連結するケースを練習しましょう。
2語ですが、まるで1語のように聞こえます。1語のように聞こえた瞬間に、元の2語が思い浮かぶようになるのが目標です。

✅ 頻出単語チェック！ **Listening Section**

語句と意味を品詞に気をつけながら結びつけてみましょう。

1. patient [n.] ( )
2. medicine ( )
3. exercise [v.] ( )
4. gain weight ( )
5. improve ( )
6. in good shape ( )
7. take care ( )
8. first-aid box ( )

a. a container that contains basic medical supplies
b. to become heavier (often used for people)
c. a person who is unwell or injured
d. fit and healthy
e. something that people take to get better when they are unwell
f. to be careful when doing something
g. to do activities so people stay fit and healthy
h. to get better (at something)

Listening Section

PART 1 写真描写問題　　　　　　　　　　　　　　　 1-75, 76

> *Check Point!* 　複数の人物の動作について述べる例を見てみましょう。
> They're shutting the door.

それぞれの写真について、4つの説明文の中から最も適切なものを1つずつ選びましょう。

1.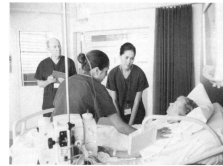

Ⓐ Ⓑ Ⓒ Ⓓ

2.

Ⓐ Ⓑ Ⓒ Ⓓ

PART 2 応答問題　　　　　　　　　　　　　　　　 1-77-81

> *Check Point!* 　How+ 形容詞で、分量や頻度、程度を問う形を覚えましょう。
> How much is a taxi to the airport?

それぞれの設問の応答として最も適切なものを1つずつ選びましょう。

3. Mark your answer on your answer sheet.　　　　Ⓐ Ⓑ Ⓒ

4. Mark your answer on your answer sheet.　　　　Ⓐ Ⓑ Ⓒ

5. Mark your answer on your answer sheet.　　　　Ⓐ Ⓑ Ⓒ

6. Mark your answer on your answer sheet.　　　　Ⓐ Ⓑ Ⓒ

7. Mark your answer on your answer sheet.　　　　Ⓐ Ⓑ Ⓒ

PART 3 会話問題

 1-82, 83

Check Point! 「どこで交わされている会話か」場面を聞き取りましょう。
Where most likely is this conversation taking place?

会話についての設問に対し、最も適切なものを１つずつ選びましょう。

8. Where most likely is this conversation taking place?
   (A) At a gym
   (B) In a restaurant
   (C) In a hospital
   (D) At a bicycle store

9. What does the woman say about the man?
   (A) He has gained weight.
   (B) He is exercising more.
   (C) He has improved his health.
   (D) He takes the train to work.

10. What does the woman ask the man to do?
    (A) Try to come up with a better plan
    (B) Be careful when riding his bicycle
    (C) Eat less instead of riding a bicycle
    (D) Not travel to work during rush hour

PART 4 説明文問題

 1-84, 85

Check Point! 「聞き手は誰か」を問う形を知っておきましょう。
Who most likely are the listeners?

説明文についての設問に対し、最も適切なものを１つずつ選びましょう。

11. Who most likely are the listeners?
    (A) Hospital staff
    (B) Company doctors
    (C) Company employees
    (D) Health check nurses

12. What will happen tomorrow afternoon?
    (A) A meeting will be held on the 10th floor.
    (B) An e-mail announcement will be made.
    (C) A late lunch will be served to employees.
    (D) Doctors and nurses will check employees' health.

13. What will be provided in two weeks?
    (A) The results of the health check
    (B) Another employee health check
    (C) Answers to employee questions
    (D) Instructions from doctors and nurses

■形容詞の中でも最も多く出題されるのが数量形容詞です。数えられる名詞（可算名詞）の**数**の多少と、数えられない名詞（不可算名詞）の量の多少を区別しましょう。

① **many** と **much**：可算名詞を修飾するのは many で、不可算名詞には much が使われます。

many は数の多いこと、much は量の多いことを表します。

→ many cars / cats / years

→ much water / snow / food

《例題》各空所に入れるべき最も適切な語を 1 つ選んで、その記号を書きなさい。

1. The meeting room was full with ------- attendants.

    (A) any   (B) much   (C) many   (D) every

---

② **(a) few** と **(a) little**：few は数が少ない、little は量が少ないことを表します。

それぞれ不定冠詞 a が付けば肯定的な意味となり、「少しはいる／ある」となります。

a がなければ否定的な意味となり、「ほとんどない」となります。

---

2. We had very ------- snow last winter.

    (A) few   (B) many   (C) several   (D) little

Reading Section

✓ 頻出単語チェック！ Reading Section

語句と意味を品詞に気をつけながら結びつけてみましょう。

1. accident (　　)

2. exhausted (　　)

3. general affairs (　　)

4. remind (　　)

5. demonstration (　　)

6. workout [n.] (　　)

7. treatment (　　)

8. in partnership with (　　)

a. actions taken to try to cure a disease or health problem

b. relating to management and administration

c. an unexpected event that often causes injury

d. some exercise

e. very tired

f. showing someone how to do something

g. to tell people something to help them remember it

h. working closely together with

PART 5 短文穴埋め問題

Check Point! 文法問題：数量形容詞、語彙問題：形容詞
形容詞の後が可算名詞か不可算名詞かを見極めましょう。

それぞれの空所に入れるのに最も適切なものを1つずつ選びましょう。

14. The doctor told Sue that it's important for her to do ------- exercise every day.
(A) any
(B) many
(C) a few
(D) a little   Ⓐ Ⓑ Ⓒ Ⓓ

15. Greg doesn't eat ------- healthy meals at lunch time, because he often has fast food.
(A) most
(B) none
(C) little
(D) many   Ⓐ Ⓑ Ⓒ Ⓓ

16. After her accident last week, Jane had to spend ------- nights in the hospital.
(A) any
(B) each
(C) much
(D) several   Ⓐ Ⓑ Ⓒ Ⓓ

17. My cold was so bad yesterday that I felt ------- after just a 10-minute walk.
(A) cured
(B) offensive
(C) exhausted
(D) contained   Ⓐ Ⓑ Ⓒ Ⓓ

18. My doctor warned me that ------- drinking and overeating is bad for my health.
(A) frequent
(B) capable
(C) convenient
(D) memorable   Ⓐ Ⓑ Ⓒ Ⓓ

Check Point!

語彙問題：接続詞（句）
文章挿入問題：空所が段落の最後なら段落の結びを選びましょう。

それぞれの空所に入れるのに最も適切なものを1つずつ選びましょう。

✉ E-MAIL

To:	All employees
From:	General Affairs Dept. <administration@well-tech.com>
Date:	Jan. 23
Subject:	Presentation about healthy eating

Dear All,

This e-mail is to remind everyone that a special lunchtime presentation will be given in the company cafeteria today. The speaker is Dr. Lydia Jameson, who will be offering advice on ways to prepare healthy meals.

As part of her presentation, Dr. Jameson is going to show participants how to cook several simple dishes. -------- the cooking demonstration, **19.** she will explain some simple exercises that you can do to stay in shape and feel better. --------. **20.**

The one-hour presentation will start at noon. There is no -------- to **21.** participate, and everyone who attends will receive a free lunch. So be sure to take advantage of this amazing opportunity.

Best regards,

Tina Murphy

---

19. (A) Whereas
   (B) Along with
   (C) Even though
   (D) Whether or not

20. (A) We require volunteers to prepare the cafeteria.
   (B) This schedule is subject to changes.
   (C) So employees are encouraged to arrive early if possible.
   (D) These include small workouts that you can do at your desk.

21. (A) charge
   (B) charges
   (C) charged
   (D) charging

文章を読んで、それぞれの設問の答えとして最も適切なものを1つずつ選びましょう。

YFG Monthly

May 14

YFG Memorial Hospital is proud to announce the opening of a new cancer research and treatment building. The new center, which will open on July 22 of this year, is funded by the Hope-Wellington Foundation for Cancer Research, in partnership with a number of local and international companies and sponsors. With the addition of this new building, YFG Memorial will likely come to be considered one of the top cancer treatment centers in the country.

Cancer treatment and research is currently performed in the East Wing of the hospital's main building. This newly vacant space will be occupied by the expansion of our emergency treatment areas, which have become overcrowded as the increase in the town's population has led to more patients.

---

22. What is the purpose of the article?

(A) To share information about a new facility

(B) To discuss advances in cancer research

(C) To thank the hospital's sponsors

(D) To announce the closure of an area

23. What is indicated about the East Wing of the hospital?

(A) It will be used for a new cancer treatment division.

(B) It is the most crowded area of the hospital.

(C) It will be used for emergency treatment facilities.

(D) It is sponsored by a foundation.

The Bank & The Post Office

⠿ *Warm up* ▸ Dictation Practice 2-01

それぞれの空所に入る語を、音声を聞いて書き入れてみましょう。

1. Since I left my mobile phone at the post office, I had to go there the
   (　　　　　) (　　　　　　　　).
2. I (　　　　　) (　　　　　　) meet you in front of the post office.
3. Do you (　　　　　) (　　　　　) I ask you to take me to the post office?
4. The deal between two banks (　　　　　) (　　　　　　) for ten years.
5. Our new manager will come (　　　　　) (　　　　　).
6. The post office is quite (　　　　　) (　　　　　) from my apartment.
7. I would like to (　　　　　) (　　　　　) our new financial services today.
8. I (　　　　　) (　　　　　) would open a new account at our bank.
9. She is interested in learning (　　　　　) (　　　　　) the Japanese
   banking system.
10. I'm not satisfied (　　　　　) (　　　　　) service at the post office.

> ### 🔍 Points to Dictate
> 引き続き、前の語の最後の音が次の語の最初の音と連結するケースを練習し
> ましょう。子音＋子音、子音＋母音の両方のケースが含まれています。1語
> のように聞こえた瞬間に元の2語が思い浮かぶようになるのが目標です。

✔ 頻出単語チェック！ Listening Section

語句と意味を品詞に気をつけながら結びつけてみましょう。

1. withdraw (　　)　　　　　**a.** to send something by mail
2. mail [v.] (　　)　　　　　**b.** to take money out of the bank
3. package [n.] (　　)　　　　**c.** to say no to something
4. business day (　　)　　　　**d.** to start using a bank to keep your money
5. open an account (　　)　　　**e.** an item that is sent by mail or delivery company
6. deposit [v.] (　　)　　　　**f.** a workday between Monday and Friday
7. reject [v.] (　　)　　　　　**g.** something that you must do
8. requirement (　　)　　　　**h.** to put money into a bank

| PART 1 | 写真描写問題 | 2-02, 03 |

> ***Check Point!*** 複数の人物の動作について述べる例を見てみましょう。
> Some people are paying at a cashier.

それぞれの写真について、4つの説明文の中から最も適切なものを1つずつ選びましょう。

1.

Ⓐ Ⓑ Ⓒ Ⓓ

2.

Ⓐ Ⓑ Ⓒ Ⓓ

| PART 2 | 応答問題 | 2-04-08 |

> ***Check Point!*** How+ 副詞で、所要時間、頻度、距離を尋ねる形を覚えましょう。
> How often do you play tennis?

それぞれの設問の応答として最も適切なものを1つずつ選びましょう。

3. Mark your answer on your answer sheet.   Ⓐ Ⓑ Ⓒ

4. Mark your answer on your answer sheet.   Ⓐ Ⓑ Ⓒ

5. Mark your answer on your answer sheet.   Ⓐ Ⓑ Ⓒ

6. Mark your answer on your answer sheet.   Ⓐ Ⓑ Ⓒ

7. Mark your answer on your answer sheet.   Ⓐ Ⓑ Ⓒ

PART 3　会話問題

2-09, 10

「話者はどのような職業に就いているか」を聞き取りましょう。
Where do the speakers most likely work?

会話についての設問に対し、最も適切なものを1つずつ選びましょう。

8. Where do the speakers most likely
work?
(A) In a bank
(B) In a passport office
(C) At a travel agency
(D) At a department store

9. Why does the woman ask for help?
(A) A customer has lost his passport.
(B) A person from another country
wants to open an account.
(C) She doesn't have enough
money.
(D) The man rejected the application.

10. What does the man ask the woman
to do?
(A) Explain the rule to the customer
(B) Tell the customer to visit another
bank
(C) Ask the customer if he is a
resident
(D) Open an account for the
customer

PART 4　説明文問題

 2-11, 12

Check Point!

アナウンスが「どこで聞かれるか」を聞き取りましょう。
Where is this announcement taking place?

説明文についての設問に対し、最も適切なものを1つずつ選びましょう。

11. Where is this announcement taking
place?
(A) A bank
(B) A post office
(C) A stationery shop
(D) A department store

12. What is the problem?
(A) There are a lot of customers.
(B) There are too few stamps.
(C) The credit card machine is
broken.
(D) The entrance is crowded.

13. What does the speaker ask listeners
to do?
(A) Join the fast lane to buy stamps
(B) Wait near the entrance
(C) Pay with a credit card
(D) Fill out paperwork before their
turn

Grammar Review　自動詞と他動詞

■英語に自信がある人でも間違えてしまうのが、自動詞と他動詞の使い分けです。自動詞と他動詞の違いは目的語を取るか取らないかで、動詞の直後に前置詞が必要か否かで区別します。

①**自動詞（動詞 + 前置詞）**：wait for 〜（〜を待つ）、graduate from 〜（〜を卒業する）など

《例題》各空所に入れるべき最も適切な語句を1つ選んで、その記号を書きなさい。

1. We ------- London very late at night.
   (A) arrived　　(B) arrived in　　(C) arrived for　　(D) arrived on

②**他動詞（動詞 + 目的語）**：leave 〜（〜を去る）、marry 〜（〜と結婚する）など

2. We ------- a wide range of political issues.
   (A) discussed　　　(B) discussed about　　　(C) discussed on
   (D) discussed with

◎上の arrive（自動詞）や discuss（他動詞）のように、自動詞のみあるいは他動詞のみしかないという動詞は実際にはそれほど多くありません。多くの動詞は自・他両方の形で使われます。

3. She finally ------- five o'clock this afternoon.
   (A) appeared　　(B) appeared in　　(C) appeared for　　(D) appeared at

Reading Section

✔ 頻出単語チェック!　Reading Section

語句と意味を品詞に気をつけながら結びつけてみましょう。

1. the postal service (　　)
2. reasonable (　　)
3. regret [v.] (　　)
4. provide (　　)
5. unsuccessful (　　)
6. branch [n.] (　　)
7. balance [n.] (　　)
8. domestic (　　)

a. an office or shop that is one of many owned by a large company
b. did not succeed; failed
c. the organization that delivers people's mail
d. the amount of money in a bank account
e. within the country; not international
f. to give someone something that they need
g. good value
h. to be sorry about something that you did

PART 5　短文穴埋め問題

文法問題：自動詞と他動詞、語彙問題：形容詞
自動詞・他動詞の見極めには、目的語を取るかどうかに注目しましょう。

それぞれの空所に入れるのに最も適切なものを1つずつ選びましょう。

14. Do you know if the postal service in this country ------- mail on weekends?
(A) delivers
(B) delivers to
(C) delivers for
(D) delivers with　Ⓐ Ⓑ Ⓒ Ⓓ

15. Steven ------- the bank, but when he got there it was already closed.
(A) ran
(B) ran to
(C) ran by
(D) ran into　Ⓐ Ⓑ Ⓒ Ⓓ

16. There was a long line of people ------- the post office this morning to mail packages.
(A) waiting
(B) waiting at
(C) waiting for
(D) waiting with　Ⓐ Ⓑ Ⓒ Ⓓ

17. The price of sending the package was only two dollars, which was much more ------- than I had expected.
(A) serious
(B) current
(C) valuable
(D) reasonable　Ⓐ Ⓑ Ⓒ Ⓓ

18. The bank's ------- report will be released next week.
(A) annual
(B) reverse
(C) identical
(D) extensive　Ⓐ Ⓑ Ⓒ Ⓓ

それぞれの空所に入れるのに最も適切なものを1つずつ選びましょう。

Dear Mr. Baker,

We ------- to inform you that your credit card application has been unsuccessful.
19.

This ------- was based on a number of factors. First, you have only had a bank
20.
account with us for six months. Usually, we prefer a person to have had an
account for at least one year before issuing them a credit card. -------. For us to
21.
provide you with a card, you would need to have at least two times the amount
of credit requested in your savings account.

Although your application has been rejected, we encourage you to apply again
in the future once you have met our requirements.

Sincerely yours,

Bill Clifton
First Federal Bank

---

19. (A) affect
(B) believe
(C) regret
(D) oversee

20. (A) decided
(B) decision
(C) deciding
(D) decisional

21. (A) Second, you can apply by
calling your local branch.
(B) Moreover, your current balance
is too low.
(C) However, those changes can
be made in special cases.
(D) I hope that you will understand
our decision.

PART 7   読解問題

Check Point!   お知らせ（1つの文書）
タイトルや図表の項目名などチェックしましょう。

文章を読んで、それぞれの設問の答えとして最も適切なものを1つずつ選びましょう。

Lake Papakoa Post Office

The new prices for domestic and international mail are listed below.

Type of Stamp	Price
Letter (standard-sized)	From $0.55
Square, Oversized, or Unusual Envelopes	From $0.75
Postcard (standard-sized, rectangular postcards)	From $0.36
International Letter (standard-sized)	From $1.20

If you are planning on sending a package, then please refer to the following price list. Please note that the prices listed here are for our standard-sized packages. For prices for packages of special sizes and shapes, please call 188-7711-2345.

Destination	Type of Service	Price
Domestic	Standard Mail (2-5 business days)	$13.45
	Express Mail (1-2 business days)	$18.75
International	Standard Mail (2-8 business days)	$22.95
	Express Mail (1-3 business days)	$29.95

22. Why was the notice posted?
    (A) To update the price lists
    (B) To explain how to send packages
    (C) To assist customers in making cost estimates
    (D) To advertise a new shipping service

23. How much is the cheapest option for sending a standard-sized package abroad?
    (A) $1.20
    (B) $13.45
    (C) $22.95
    (D) $29.95

New Products

:: Warm up | **Dictation Practice** 2-13

それぞれの空所に入る語を、音声を聞いて書き入れてみましょう。

1. I ( ) ( ) be at the client's office by 10:00.
2. I ( ) ( ) be at the client's office by 10:00.
3. I'm ( ) ( ) talk about our cutting-edge technology.
4. I'm ( ) ( ) talk about our cutting-edge technology.
5. He ( ) ( ) ( ) go to Australia to sell their new product.
6. He ( ) ( ) ( ) go to Australia to sell their new product.
7. We ( ) ( ) make some slides to describe our brand-new product.
8. He ( ) ( ) complete his sales report on new products by noon.
9. She ( ) ( ) change her sales plan because of the bad economy.
10. Ken's ( ) ( ) work with a client he doesn't like.

Q Points to Dictate

音の連結と脱落が起こり、元の単語の音とは全く異なる音のように聞こえる例です。1〜6は同じ文章を2通りで発話していますので、よく聞き比べてみましょう。どちらも聞いた時に分かるようにしておきましょう。

✓ 頻出単語チェック！ **Listening Section**

語句と意味を品詞に気をつけながら結びつけてみましょう。

1. look at ( )
2. overseas ( )
3. commercial [n.] ( )
4. marketing ( )
5. broadcast [v.] ( )
6. produce [v.] ( )
7. safely ( )
8. brochure ( )

a. to send a TV or radio show to people's homes
b. in a safe way
c. to make
d. promoting the product to people
e. a short video to promote a product
f. to watch
g. a booklet with information about a product or service
h. in another country

Listening Section

PART 1　写真描写問題　🔊 2-14, 15

> *Check Point!* 　複数のうちの1人の動作について述べる例を見てみましょう。
> A man is talking to some women.

それぞれの写真について、4つの説明文の中から最も適切なものを1つずつ選びましょう。

1.

Ⓐ Ⓑ Ⓒ Ⓓ

2.

Ⓐ Ⓑ Ⓒ Ⓓ

PART 2　応答問題　🔊 2-16-20

> *Check Point!* 　Why で始まるが、理由を尋ねる疑問文ではないことに注意しましょう。
> Why don't you tell us about your new job?

それぞれの設問の応答として最も適切なものを1つずつ選びましょう。

3. Mark your answer on your answer sheet.　Ⓐ Ⓑ Ⓒ

4. Mark your answer on your answer sheet.　Ⓐ Ⓑ Ⓒ

5. Mark your answer on your answer sheet.　Ⓐ Ⓑ Ⓒ

6. Mark your answer on your answer sheet.　Ⓐ Ⓑ Ⓒ

7. Mark your answer on your answer sheet.　Ⓐ Ⓑ Ⓒ

Check Point! 「話者がどのような職業についているか」を聞き取りましょう。
In what area do the speakers work?

会話についての設問に対し、最も適切なものを 1 つずつ選びましょう。

8. In what area do the speakers work?
(A) Sales
(B) Product design
(C) Marketing
(D) Accounting

9. What is the woman concerned about?
(A) The man will not like her idea.
(B) The design is not interesting.
(C) Production is not fast enough.
(D) The car may not be cheap enough.

10. What does the man suggest?
(A) Lowering the price of the car
(B) Producing more cars
(C) Using cheaper parts
(D) Changing the size of the engine

Check Point! 「話し手がどこで働いているか」を問う形を知っておきましょう。
Where does the speaker work?

説明文についての設問に対し、最も適切なものを 1 つずつ選びましょう。

11. Where does the speaker work?
(A) At a car magazine company
(B) At a newspaper company
(C) At a car company
(D) At the city office

12. What does the speaker say about the car?
(A) It is easier to drive than to park.
(B) It is too small for four passengers.
(C) It is the company's smallest model.
(D) It is made for city driving, not freeways.

13. What will the listeners most likely do next?
(A) Test drive the car
(B) Check the luggage space
(C) Look at the engine
(D) Read some information

Grammar Review　接尾辞と品詞—形容詞

■どの接尾辞がどの品詞を作るか、ということを知っていると、1つの語幹からすぐに4つ、5つと語彙の知識が広がります。ここでは形容詞を作る接尾辞を見てみましょう。

例えば、comfort は名詞（安楽、慰め）と動詞（〈人を〉慰める）として使用されます。comfort という語幹に、-able という接尾辞を付けると comfortable（快適な）という形容詞が誕生します。

■形容詞を作る接尾辞の例

-al (actual), -ant (defendant), -ar (regular), -an (vegetarian), -ative (creative),
-ive (active), -less (careless), -logical (biological), etc.

《例題》各空所に入れるべき最も適切な語を1つ選んで、その記号を書きなさい。

1. My grandfather likes this ------- sofa.
   (A) comfort　　(B) comfortable　　(C) comfortably　　(D) comfortability

2. Please keep your personal belongings in your ------- locker.
   (A) individualism　　(B) individually　　(C) individualise　　(D) individual

Reading Section

☑ 頻出単語チェック！　Reading Section

語句と意味を品詞に気をつけながら結びつけてみましょう。

1. develop (　　)
2. in spite of (　　)
3. model (　　)
4. the majority of (　　)
5. specialize (　　)
6. function [n.] (　　)
7. rechargeable (　　)
8. properly (　　)

a. in the correct way
b. to create and make
c. without being affected by
d. can have its power restored by plugging it in
e. a particular type of machine or device
f. to focus on a specific topic or use
g. most
h. a useful thing that a computer or electronic device can do

それぞれの空所に入れるのに最も適切なものを 1 つずつ選びましょう。

14. This new electronic device looks very -------.
(A) use
(B) useful
(C) usefully
(D) used
Ⓐ Ⓑ Ⓒ Ⓓ

15. More and more automakers around the world are developing ------- cars.
(A) electric
(B) electrician
(C) electricity
(D) electrical
Ⓐ Ⓑ Ⓒ Ⓓ

16. After the success of our new product, we had a very ------- team dinner to celebrate.
(A) enjoy
(B) enjoying
(C) enjoyable
(D) enjoyment
Ⓐ Ⓑ Ⓒ Ⓓ

17. Our company ------- is developing ten new products that will be sold next year.
(A) currently
(B) gratefully
(C) frequently
(D) particularly
Ⓐ Ⓑ Ⓒ Ⓓ

18. This computer is priced ------- higher than the old model, but it is much faster.
(A) slightly
(B) openly
(C) instantly
(D) efficiently
Ⓐ Ⓑ Ⓒ Ⓓ

Check Point!　語彙問題：複数の品詞（接続詞・副詞・前置詞）
文章挿入問題:空所が文末なら結びとして適切な文を選びましょう。

それぞれの空所に入れるのに最も適切なものを1つずつ選びましょう。

XF-A4500

The XF-A4500 electronic Japanese-English dictionary is 15 percent smaller than our previous models. ------ **19.** its smaller size, this new dictionary is much more powerful than the majority of similar products on the market. It contains all of the dictionaries included in previous models, plus several new ones. (See the separate sheet for the full list of dictionaries.)

New features also include works of literature, specialized encyclopedias for history and science, and ------ **20.** for studying English and Japanese. On top of this, the dictionary is easier to use than before thanks to its new touch screen, which can be operated with your finger or using a special stylus pen. ------ **21.**.

XF-A4500

---

19. (A) As if
(B) Once
(C) Mostly
(D) In spite of

20. (A) functions
(B) functional
(C) functioning
(D) functionally

21. (A) This has been proven with scientific tests.
(B) Please refer to your manual for further details.
(C) And this price is only available until May 10th.
(D) See our Web site for more details.

文章を読んで、それぞれの設問の答えとして最も適切なものを1つずつ選びましょう。

Important Notice

We regret to inform our customers of a problem with the rechargeable battery in our new OS459-x digital camera. Unfortunately, the batteries that were shipped during the month of February are not functioning properly. The batteries should last for six hours after being charged, but these batteries are only lasting for three hours on average.

Any customer who has a problem with the battery for the OS459-x should contact us. We will replace the battery with a new one for free. Also, to make up for the inconvenience caused, we will provide customers affected with a $20 gift certificate that can be used to purchase any of our camera products or accessories.

We sincerely apologize for this error.

---

22. What is being announced?
(A) A new digital camera
(B) A gift certificate for new customers
(C) A problem with a battery
(D) A special offer for a new product

23. What are customers being asked to do?
(A) Charge the batteries for six hours
(B) Contact the company for a replacement
(C) Purchase a $20 gift certificate
(D) Buy a new battery for the OS459-x

Travel

:: ***Warm up***	**Dictation Practice**	2-25

それぞれの空所に入る語を、音声を聞いて書き入れてみましょう。省略形も1語として書き入れましょう。

1. A: Is this your (1.　　　　) (2.　　　　) in Spain?

　　 B: No, (3.　　　　) (4.　　　　) here twice before.

2. A: Excuse me, (1.　　　　) (2.　　　　) would like to (3.　　　　) (4.　　　　) flight reservation.

　　 B: Sure. Could I (5.　　　　) (6.　　　　) name please?

3. A: Do we also (1.　　　　) (2.　　　　) buy a ticket for a child under six?

　　 B: No, you don't (3.　　　　)(4.　　　　).

4. A: What (1.　　　　) (2.　　　　) food did they serve you on the airplane?

　　 B: (3.　　　　) (4.　　　　) mainly Japanese dishes.

5. A: (1.　　　　) (2.　　　　) (3.　　　　) going to have for lunch at the airport?

　　 B: (4.　　　　) (5.　　　　) (6.　　　　) try that new Chinese restaurant?

> 🔍 **Points to Dictate**
>
> Part 2 と同じ対話文形式になっています。今までに練習してきた音の変化が複数入り、徐々に空所の数が増えてきていますので頑張って聞き取りましょう。

✔ 頻出単語チェック！	**Listening Section**

語句と意味を品詞に気をつけながら結びつけてみましょう。

1. take a nap (　)
a. a place

2. suite (　)
b. a choice

3. upgrade [v.] (　)
c. to change to a better thing

4. make a decision (　)
d. to make a choice

5. landmark [n.] (　)
e. instructions for how to go to a place

6. option (　)
f. a well-known building or place

7. direction (　)
g. connected rooms in a hotel (for example, living room and bedroom)

8. location (　)
h. to have a short sleep

Listening Section

PART 1	写真描写問題	2-26, 27

> ***Check Point!*** 　男性か女性どちらか1人の動作について述べる例を見てみましょう。
> A woman is eating lunch.

それぞれの写真について、4つの説明文の中から最も適切なものを1つずつ選びましょう。

1.

(A) (B) (C) (D)

2.

(A) (B) (C) (D)

PART 2	応答問題	2-28-32

> ***Check Point!*** 　一般疑問文は5W1Hの疑問文に次いで多く出題されます。
> Do you sell road maps?

それぞれの設問の応答として最も適切なものを1つずつ選びましょう。

3. Mark your answer on your answer sheet.　　(A) (B) (C)

4. Mark your answer on your answer sheet.　　(A) (B) (C)

5. Mark your answer on your answer sheet.　　(A) (B) (C)

6. Mark your answer on your answer sheet.　　(A) (B) (C)

7. Mark your answer on your answer sheet.　　(A) (B) (C)

PART 3 会話問題 2-33, 34

Check Point! 「話者が３人いること」を聞き取りましょう。
What do the two women want to do?

会話についての設問に対し、最も適切なものを１つずつ選びましょう。

8. What do the women want to do?
(A) Book a hotel room
(B) Buy tickets to an event
(C) Go somewhere for the weekend
(D) Look for a suite room

9. What does the man offer to do?
(A) Give them a discount
(B) Give them an extra night for free
(C) Pay for their evening meal
(D) Upgrade their booking

10. What does the woman mean when she says, "That'll do"?
(A) She has no other options.
(B) The offer is acceptable.
(C) She will continue looking.
(D) She cannot make a decision.

PART 4 説明文問題 2-35, 36

Check Point! 話者が "------" と言ったのはどういう意図か、前後関係から考えましょう。
What does the man mean when he says, "------"?

説明文についての設問に対し、最も適切なものを１つずつ選びましょう。

11. Where does the man most likely work?
(A) At a tour company
(B) At a car rental company
(C) At a hotel
(D) At an information center

12. What does the man mean when he says, "That's how you get hold of me"?
(A) He is holding the keys to the car.
(B) He can be reached using that phone number.
(C) He wants the listener to hold a map.
(D) He can repeat this information.

13. What does the man ask the listener to do?
(A) Call him at 5:00 P.M.
(B) Stop at a nearby gas station
(C) Visit some famous landmarks
(D) Return before a certain time

Grammar Review　接尾辞と品詞—副詞

■どの接尾辞がどの品詞を作るか、ということを知っていると、1つの語幹からすぐに4つ、5つと語彙の知識が広がります。ここでは副詞を作る接尾辞を見てみましょう。
例えば、final という形容詞（最後の）に、-ly という接尾辞を付けると finally（最後に）という副詞が誕生します。

■副詞を作る接尾辞の例
　-ably, -ibly, -bly (prob*ably*), -handed (left*handed*), -ically (crit*ically*),
　-ly (final*ly*), -ward, -wards, -ways (after*ward*), -wise (like*wise*), etc.

《例題》各空所に入れるべき最も適切な語を1つ選んで、その記号を書きなさい。

1. It will ------- rain tomorrow.
   (A) probable　　(B) probably　　(C) probability　　(D) probabilistic

2. Three passengers were ------- injured in the accident.
   (A) critic　　(B) critical　　(C) critically　　(D) criticise

Reading Section

✅ 頻出単語チェック!　Reading Section

語句と意味を品詞に気をつけながら結びつけてみましょう。

1. frequently (　　)
2. due to (　　)
3. reduce (　　)
4. end up (　　)
5. interruption (　　)
6. inconvenience [n.] (　　)
7. estimate [n.] (　　)
8. purchase [v.] (　　)

a. something that causes a short stop to something happening
b. because of
c. a guess
d. to lower the amount or number of something
e. to buy
f. often
g. trouble that causes something to be difficult or take longer
h. to do something that you did not plan to do

PART 5 短文穴埋め問題

それぞれの空所に入れるのに最も適切なものを1つずつ選びましょう。

14. People ------- think that the trains here are unreliable, but that's not true.
    (A) generally
    (B) generalize
    (C) generalized
    (D) general
    Ⓐ Ⓑ Ⓒ Ⓓ

15. -------, the cost of the train from London to Manchester was much cheaper than the bus.
    (A) Amaze
    (B) Amazed
    (C) Amazingly
    (D) Amazing
    Ⓐ Ⓑ Ⓒ Ⓓ

16. Although we bought rail passes for our trip to Europe, we didn't end up riding trains very -------.
    (A) frequent
    (B) frequently
    (C) frequented
    (D) frequentness
    Ⓐ Ⓑ Ⓒ Ⓓ

17. According to our information, your flight to Berlin has been canceled, -------, due to heavy snow.
    (A) physically
    (B) thoughtfully
    (C) unnaturally
    (D) unfortunately
    Ⓐ Ⓑ Ⓒ Ⓓ

18. Jim ------- left his passport at home, so he could not take his flight to Tokyo this morning.
    (A) loosely
    (B) quickly
    (C) endlessly
    (D) carelessly
    Ⓐ Ⓑ Ⓒ Ⓓ

Check Point!
語彙問題：名詞
文章挿入問題：空所が段落の最後なら段落の結びを選びましょう。

それぞれの空所に入れるのに最も適切なものを1つずつ選びましょう。

Web Page

← → ↻ ⌂ ⊕ www.citytrainservice.com | Q

CHANGES TO OUR REGULAR SERVICE

Due to the heavy snowfall yesterday, the number of trains has been reduced today, including the cancellation of all express train services.
19. .

We expect the trains to be ------ throughout the day as a result of the
20.
limited service. If at all possible, we recommend that you avoid traveling until tomorrow, when our regular services are expected to resume.

In addition to the limited service, the following stations will be temporarily closed: Clinton Street, Fulton, Park Ridge, and Division. These stations will be re-opened as soon as the snow has been removed from the surrounding areas. According to current ------, they should be in
21.
operation again by noon today.

We apologize for the inconvenience and ask for your understanding. Please visit this Web site regularly for updates on the situation.

---

19. (A) Please be sure to study the process described below.
(B) We are taking these measures for the sake of our passengers' safety.
(C) Heavy damage is expected due to the coming storm.
(D) These interruptions were scheduled after careful planning.

20. (A) crowd
(B) crowds
(C) crowded
(D) crowding

21. (A) conclusions
(B) estimates
(C) weather
(D) cooperation

Check Point!

インフォメーション（1つの文書）
何の情報か、特徴的な情報は何かに注目しましょう。

文章を読んで、それぞれの設問の答えとして最も適切なものを1つずつ選びましょう。

Rail Passes in France

The French Rail Pass is the best way to discover France. Passes are for one week, ten days, or one month. Each pass allows unlimited travel on all intercity trains, including the high-speed TGV trains. The passes, which are only available to foreign tourists, can be purchased at selected travel agencies. —[1]—. In order to buy a pass, customers must present a valid passport with an active, short-term tourist visa. —[2]—. When boarding or booking trains, passengers must present both their passport and rail pass together. The name of the passenger must always match the name listed on the ticket. —[3]—. If you plan to ride the train almost every day, the train pass will be the most affordable option. —[4]—. Otherwise, it may be cheaper to purchase separate tickets for each trip.

22. What is the purpose of the information?
   (A) To explain about rail passes in France
   (B) To describe the French train system
   (C) To convince someone to buy a train pass
   (D) To present the history of the French Rail Pass

23. In which of the positions marked [1], [2], [3] and [4] does the following sentence best belong?
   "They are also available at train stations across France."
   (A) [1]
   (B) [2]
   (C) [3]
   (D) [4]

Daily Life

Dictation Practice 2-37

それぞれの空所に入る語を、音声を聞いて書き入れてみましょう。

Woman: ABC Hotel. How may I (1.   ) (2.   )?

    Man: Hello. I'd like to (3.   ) (4.   ) (5.   ).

Woman: Certainly. (6.   ) (7.   ) would you like?

    Man: Two (8.   ) (9.   ) April first.

Woman: Certainly. (10.   ) (11.   ) like a single room or a double room?

    Man: A single room. What's (12.   ) (13.   ) for the room?

Woman: Our single (14.   ) (15.   ) 100 dollars per night, so your total

        (16.   ) (17.   ) 200 dollars. Would you like (18.   )

        (19.   ) (20.   ) the room for you?

    Man: Yes, please.

 Points to Dictate

Part 3 形式のやや長い対話文の中で起こる音の変化にチャレンジしてみましょう。ナチュラルスピードの流れに耳がついていけるようになっていますか。音声は複数回聞いても構いません。

☑ 頻出単語チェック! **Listening Section**

語句と意味を品詞に気をつけながら結びつけてみましょう。

1. vehicle (　　)
2. housework (　　)
3. plumber (　　)
4. pick up (　　)
5. repair [v.] (　　)
6. definitely (　　)
7. otherwise (　　)
8. invite [v.] (　　)

a. a person that fixes bath, sinks, and showers

b. for example, a car, a truck, or a boat

c. tasks such as cleaning the house and washing clothes

d. to ask someone to do something together

e. to make something broken work again

f. if that does not happen

g. surely, certainly

h. to collect someone from a place with a car

Listening Section

PART 1　写真描写問題　2-38, 39

> **Check Point!**　2人のうちの1人の動作について述べる例を見てみましょう。
> One of the men is closing the door of the building.

それぞれの写真について、4つの説明文の中から最も適切なものを1つずつ選びましょう。

1.

Ⓐ Ⓑ Ⓒ Ⓓ

2.

Ⓐ Ⓑ Ⓒ Ⓓ

PART 2　応答問題　2-40-44

> **Check Point!**　否定疑問文には肯定なら Yes、否定なら No と答えるのが基本と考えましょう。
> Don't you need to leave soon?

それぞれの設問の応答として最も適切なものを1つずつ選びましょう。

3. Mark your answer on your answer sheet.　　Ⓐ Ⓑ Ⓒ

4. Mark your answer on your answer sheet.　　Ⓐ Ⓑ Ⓒ

5. Mark your answer on your answer sheet.　　Ⓐ Ⓑ Ⓒ

6. Mark your answer on your answer sheet.　　Ⓐ Ⓑ Ⓒ

7. Mark your answer on your answer sheet.　　Ⓐ Ⓑ Ⓒ

| **PART 3** | 会話問題 | 2-45, 46 |

Check Point! 「一方の話者が誰であるか」を聞き取りましょう。
Who is the man?

会話についての設問に対し、最も適切なものを1つずつ選びましょう。

8. Who is the man?
  (A) A teacher
  (B) A plumber
  (C) A taxi driver
  (D) A delivery driver

9. What does the woman want the man to do?
  (A) Pick up the children from school
  (B) Tell her his address
  (C) Come back home
  (D) Repair her bathtub

10. When will the man come to the woman's house?
  (A) At 2:00 P.M.
  (B) At 3:00 P.M.
  (C) At 4:00 P.M.
  (D) Tomorrow

| **PART 4** | 説明文問題 |  2-47, 48 |

Check Point! 「話し手がなぜ電話をしているのか」その理由を聞き取りましょう。
Why is the woman calling?

説明文についての設問に対し、最も適切なものを1つずつ選びましょう。

11. Why is the woman calling?
  (A) To invite Jack to a picnic
  (B) To explain the location of a picnic
  (C) To remind Jack about the picnic
  (D) To explain a change to the time of picnic

12. When is the picnic scheduled for?
  (A) 10:00 A.M.
  (B) 11:00 A.M.
  (C) 12:00 noon
  (D) 1:00 P.M.

13. What is the listener asked to do?
  (A) Make some sandwiches
  (B) Get some cakes
  (C) Bring some drinks
  (D) Buy some fruit

Grammar Review 分詞構文

■分詞構文は、通常接続詞で始まる節［＝長い］を分詞で始まる句［＝短い］で表現し、引き締まった文体にするために、書き言葉で多く用いられます。

・同時に起こったことを表す場合：（〜しながら）

I lay on the bed **thinking** about my future.（将来について考えながらベッドに横になっていた）

・動作の継続を表す場合：（〜してから）

Opening the window, she saw blue sky.（彼女は窓を開けて青い空を見た）

She opened the window **and** saw blue sky. の and を省き、先に行われた動作（opened「開けた」）の動詞を分詞にします。

・時を表す場合：（〜している時に）

Running on the street, he found a new coffee shop.（通りを走っているときに彼は新しいコーヒー店を見つけた）

While he was running on the street, he found a new coffee shop.

《例題》各空所に入れるべき最も適切な語句を1つ選んで、その記号を書きなさい。

1. I sat on the bench ------- my favorite magazine.

   (A) read　　(B) being read　　(C) reading　　(D) to be read

2. ------- her room, she saw somebody had cleaned it.

   (A) Entering　　(B) Enter　　(C) Entered　　(D) To enter

Reading Section

✔ 頻出単語チェック!　Reading Section

語句と意味を品詞に気をつけながら結びつけてみましょう。

1. pack [v.] (　　)
2. spill [v.] (　　)
3. confirm (　　)
4. costly (　　)
5. opposite (　　)
6. look forward to (　　)
7. exhibition (　　)
8. gallery (　　)

a. an event where people can see art
b. a building where people can see art
c. to put things in a bag (for a trip)
d. to prove something that someone thought was true
e. to feel happy about something that will happen in the future
f. on the other side of the road
g. expensive
h. to cause a liquid to fall out of a container

それぞれの空所に入れるのに最も適切なものを1つずつ選びましょう。

14. He got dressed and packed his bag, ------- about all the things he had to do today.
    (A) think
    (B) thought
    (C) thinking
    (D) thinks
    Ⓐ Ⓑ Ⓒ Ⓓ

15. ------- the morning news on TV, Nancy quickly ate her breakfast and drank her tea.
    (A) Watch
    (B) Watched
    (C) Watching
    (D) Watches
    Ⓐ Ⓑ Ⓒ Ⓓ

16. ------- by the news about the company, Tim spilled his coffee all over the table.
    (A) Surprise
    (B) Surprised
    (C) Surprising
    (D) Surprises
    Ⓐ Ⓑ Ⓒ Ⓓ

17. ------- the guests at the party were some of my friends from high school.
    (A) Among
    (B) Within
    (C) From
    (D) Above
    Ⓐ Ⓑ Ⓒ Ⓓ

18. I always forget my parents' birthdays ------- putting a reminder in my calendar.
    (A) despite
    (B) between
    (C) with
    (D) until
    Ⓐ Ⓑ Ⓒ Ⓓ

PART 6 長文穴埋め問題

Check Point!

語彙問題：形容詞
文章挿入問題：空所が段落の最初なら直後の文とのつながりを
重視しましょう。

それぞれの空所に入れるのに最も適切なものを１つずつ選びましょう。

✉ E-MAIL

To:	Jill Stevens <j-stevens@freemail.com>
From:	James Cassidy <cassidy@cassidyhair.com>
Date:	March 30
Subject:	Reservation confirmed

Dear Jill,

Thank you for your call this morning.

I am writing to confirm the details of your appointment with us. I've booked you in with Tom at 11:30 on Saturday morning.

------ **19.** We're on Park Road, opposite the church. You can park outside the salon or there are ------ **20.** buses between the city hall and the church. You could also take a taxi from the train station – taxis cost about 10 dollars.

Please ask if you have any questions. We look forward to ------ **21.** you on Saturday.

Kind regards,

James Cassidy

---

19. (A) Since this is your first visit, let me tell you how to find us.
(B) We always enjoy seeing you at the salon.
(C) You asked for some information about prices.
(D) We provide several services at the salon.

20. (A) frequent
(B) costly
(C) obvious
(D) early

21. (A) see
(B) sees
(C) saw
(D) seeing

> *Check Point!* お知らせとEメール（2つの文書）
> それぞれの文書の目的や関係性を大きく捉えましょう。

文章を読んで、それぞれの設問の答えとして最も適切なものを1つずつ選びましょう。

Art Exhibition for Local Painter

A fantastic new exhibition of the works of Gregory Martin will be held at the Moorside Art Gallery next month. Martin lives locally and is well known for his beautiful paintings of the sea, but this exhibition is all about flowers. The exhibition will feature 20 new paintings and will run from March 12 to April 14.

The Gallery, which opened last year, is on Station Road, opposite the park. It features the work of local artists and offers classes for local people.

- **Entrance:** $10.00 for adults, $5.00 for seniors and children
- **Painting classes:** $8.00 for adults, $4.00 for seniors and children
- **Events (presentations, lectures, etc.):** $12.00 for adults, $6.00 for seniors and children

---

E-MAIL

To:	Linda Shaw <lindashaw@citymail.com>
From:	Helena Waters <h.waters@mymail.com>
Date:	February 15
Subject:	Exhibition

Hi Linda,

How are you? Hope work is OK.

Remember those fantastic paintings of the sea that we saw in the cafe by the beach last month? Well, that artist is having an exhibition at the Moorside Art Gallery next month. Want to go?

Tickets go on sale next week, so we should get some before it sells out. The artist is actually giving a presentation on March 14th, but I'm away on business then unfortunately. So how about we go the day after? Molly wants to come too since she doesn't have elementary school on that day.

Let me know if you'd like to go and I'll get the tickets.

Best regards,

Helena

22. What is indicated about Gregory Martin?
    (A) He is a famous local artist.
    (B) He often paints pictures of flowers.
    (C) He runs every morning.
    (D) He lives on Station Road.

23. According to the Gallery Information, what is true about Moorside Art Gallery?
    (A) It is by the beach.
    (B) It is closing next month.
    (C) It offers painting classes.
    (D) It is run by a local artist.

24. How much will Helena pay for her daughter's ticket?
    (A) $5
    (B) $6
    (C) $10
    (D) $12

UNIT 12

Job Applications

Warm up — Dictation Practice 2-49

それぞれの空所に入る語を、音声を聞いて書き入れてみましょう。

I saw your (1.   ) (2.   ) in the newspaper yesterday and I would like to apply for the (3.   ) (4.   ) personnel manager. I have over ten years of experience working in the personnel (5.   ) (6.   ) a major international company, where I was mainly (7.   ) (8.   ) (9.   ) hiring. Thanks to this experience I have become skilled at (10.   ) (11.   ) (12.   ) outstanding individuals. More details on my career history are (13.   ) (14.   ) my resume. I hope that you will (15.   ) (16.   ) (17.   ) opportunity to meet you for an interview. Thank you very much for taking time out of your busy schedule to read this letter.

Points to Dictate

Part 4 形式のやや長い文章の聞き取りにトライします。求人広告に対する応募者からの文章です。空所を埋める時には、音声だけではなく、前後関係や文法の知識も総動員して埋めるようにします。

☑ 頻出単語チェック！ Listening Section

語句と意味を品詞に気をつけながら結びつけてみましょう。

1. resume [n.] (   )
2. full-time (   )
3. part-time (   )
4. position [n.] (   )
5. opportunity (   )
6. require (   )
7. go over (   )
8. application (   )

a. a job
b. a chance to do something good
c. a document showing a person's education and employment history
d. to need
e. to look at something carefully
f. an official request for something (for example, a job)
g. not working every day or working only a few hours each day
h. working 35 to 40 hours per week

80

Listening Section

2-50, 51

| PART 1 | 写真描写問題 |

> *Check Point!* 複数のうちの1人の動作について述べる例を見てみましょう。
> A man is writing his application form.

それぞれの写真について、4つの説明文の中から最も適切なものを1つずつ選びましょう。

1.

Ⓐ Ⓑ Ⓒ Ⓓ

2.
Ⓐ Ⓑ Ⓒ Ⓓ

| PART 2 | 応答問題 |

2-52-56

> *Check Point!* A or B の疑問文には A や B で答えない解答方法も頭に入れて
> おきましょう。
> Does she want to work in Paris or London?

それぞれの設問の応答として最も適切なものを1つずつ選びましょう。

3. Mark your answer on your answer sheet.   Ⓐ Ⓑ Ⓒ

4. Mark your answer on your answer sheet.   Ⓐ Ⓑ Ⓒ

5. Mark your answer on your answer sheet.   Ⓐ Ⓑ Ⓒ

6. Mark your answer on your answer sheet.   Ⓐ Ⓑ Ⓒ

7. Mark your answer on your answer sheet.   Ⓐ Ⓑ Ⓒ

> *Check Point!* 「なぜ電話しているのか」その目的を聞き取りましょう。
> Why is the woman calling?

会話についての設問に対し、最も適切なものを1つずつ選びましょう。

8. Why is the woman calling?
(A) To explain a new opportunity
(B) To discuss an interview
(C) To make an appointment
(D) To confirm an appointment

9. What does the man mean when he says, "I'll have to go over everything with my wife"?
(A) He will try to convince his wife.
(B) He will ask for his wife's permission.
(C) He and his wife will review the information.

(D) He will need to travel with his wife.

10. What will likely happen next?
(A) The woman will schedule an interview.
(B) The woman will e-mail the man.
(C) The man will prepare a new resume.
(D) The man will research a company.

> *Check Point!* 「話し手がどのような企業に勤めているか」その業種を聞き取りましょう。
> What kind of company does the speaker work for?

説明文についての設問に対し、最も適切なものを1つずつ選びましょう。

11. What kind of company does the speaker work for?
(A) An illustration company
(B) A local magazine
(C) An Internet cafe
(D) A video production company

12. What does the speaker ask the listener to do?
(A) Send an e-mail
(B) Call a specific department
(C) Visit a Web page
(D) Resubmit an application

13. What does the speaker mean when he says, "we'd like to get to know you"?
(A) He wants to meet in person.
(B) He wants more information about her.
(C) He wants to see her resume.
(D) He wants to introduce himself.

Grammar Review 比較

複数のものを比べて述べる「比較」には4つの形があります。

■**比較級**：He is **taller** *than* his friend.（彼は友人より背が高い）形容詞 tall の比較級 taller を使い、than 以下と比べます。形容詞によっては than ではなく to を使って比較するものがあります。He is three years **senior** *to* her.（彼は彼女より3歳年上です）

■**最上級**：Tom is **the tallest** in his class.（Tom はクラスで最も背が高い）3つ以上のものを比べて「～の中で最も」という意味にするときは、the+ 形容詞 -est を使います。

■ **-er や -est を使わずに比較を表す形容詞**：His wife is **more famous** *than* he.（彼の奥さんは彼よりも有名だ）-er や -est を使わずに、more（～よりも）、most（～の中で最も）を使うものがあります。語尾が -ful, -less, -ive, -ing, -able, -ous などの形容詞の場合です。

■**原級**：He is *as* **rich** *as* Alice.（彼は Alice と同じくらい裕福だ）「～と同じくらい…だ」という場合に as ＋形容詞 / 副詞＋ as とします。

《例題》各空所に入れるべき最も適切な語句を1つ選んで、その記号を書きなさい。

1. Industrial marketing is easier ------- consumer marketing.
   (A) to contrast   (B) comparing with   (C) from   (D) than

2. The Antarctic icecap is the ------- supply of fresh water in the world.
   (A) large   (B) largely   (C) larger   (D) largest

3. The new hotel is the ------- of the four in town.
   (A) more expensive   (B) most expensive   (C) more expensively
   (D) most expensively

Reading Section

✅ **頻出単語チェック！** **Reading Section**

語句と意味を品詞に気をつけながら結びつけてみましょう。

1. expect (   )   **a.** to believe that something will be a certain way
2. enthusiastic (   )   **b.** a person applying for a job
3. fascinating (   )   **c.** to give someone a job
4. confident (   )   **d.** to officially ask for something
5. appoint (   )   **f.** wanting to do something
6. applicant (   )   **e.** very interesting
7. take away [v.] (   )   **g.** sure that something is true
8. apply (   )   **h.** to take with

> **Check Point!**
>
> 文法問題：比較、語彙問題：形容詞
> 比較は比較級＝ -er + than、最上級＝ the + -est を思い出しましょう。

それぞれの空所に入れるのに最も適切なものを 1 つずつ選びましょう。

14. More people are looking for jobs at banks because the salaries are among the -------.
(A) high
(B) highly
(C) higher
(D) highest

Ⓐ Ⓑ Ⓒ Ⓓ

15. The job interview yesterday was much ------- than Brian had expected.
(A) hard
(B) hardly
(C) harder
(D) hardest

Ⓐ Ⓑ Ⓒ Ⓓ

16. My friend told me that I will have a much ------- chance to find a well-paying job if I move to New York.
(A) great
(B) greater
(C) greatly
(D) greatest

Ⓐ Ⓑ Ⓒ Ⓓ

17. Becoming a university professor has become very -------, with hundreds of people applying for each job.
(A) competitive
(B) competitor
(C) compete
(D) competition

Ⓐ Ⓑ Ⓒ Ⓓ

18. We are looking for new workers who are ------- and enjoy new challenges.
(A) enthusiast
(B) enthusiasm
(C) enthusiastic
(D) enthusiastically

Ⓐ Ⓑ Ⓒ Ⓓ

PART 6　長文穴埋め問題

それぞれの空所に入れるのに最も適切なものを１つずつ選びましょう。

Dear Ms. Williams,

I am writing to thank you for the opportunity to be interviewed for the position of editorial assistant at *Win Design* magazine.

Being a long-time reader of your magazine, it was an honor to meet you. I also enjoyed having a chance to talk to some of your coworkers ------- the interview. **19.** It was fascinating to see all of the magazine staff busy putting together the latest issue. Watching everyone at work made me -------, once again, how much I **20.** want to work in the publishing industry.

I am confident that I have the skills and the attitude needed to be a successful editorial assistant, so I hope that you will consider appointing me. ------- **21.**

Sincerely yours,

Bryan Meyers

---

19. (A) among
　　 (B) except
　　 (C) following
　　 (D) underneath

20. (A) realization
　　 (B) realizing
　　 (C) realized
　　 (D) realize

21. (A) These are the applicants I am referring to.
　　 (B) Please allow me to re-submit my application.
　　 (C) You certainly would not regret it.
　　 (D) This is an unexpected position to be in.

> **Check Point!**　記事と手紙（2つの文書）
> 「何の記事か」、「その記事を踏まえた手紙の目的は何か」を大きく捉えましょう。

文章を読んで、それぞれの設問の答えとして最も適切なものを1つずつ選びましょう。

Popular Newgate Academy Teacher Is Leaving

One of the most popular teachers at Newgate Academy, Beth Morgan, will be leaving at the end of this school year. After ten years at the Academy, Beth plans to move to London, where she will be married next July. She told a reporter for the *Waterboro Times* that she is sorry to leave the school, but will take away many good memories of her time teaching history there. Beth also says that she wants to continue her teaching career in London if possible. We certainly hope that she will, for the sake of students in that city. Newgate Academy is now looking for a new history teacher. Anyone interested in applying can contact Meg Bryers at the Academy (m.bryers@newgate.org). A teaching certificate and five years of experience are required.

Dear Ms. Bryers,

I am writing to apply for the position of history teacher mentioned in the *Waterboro Times*. Please find enclosed my CV and two letters of recommendation.

I only have three years of teaching experience, but I hope you will still consider me for the position on the basis of my academic history and recommendation letters. The position seems well suited to my interests and abilities. I am also a qualified swimming and tennis instructor, so I would be able to serve as a coach for those sports if necessary.

I look forward to hearing from you.

Sincerely,

Brad Nathan

Tel: 718-907-8100
E-mail: b-nathan@quick-net.com

22. What is the main topic of the article?
    (A) The closing of Newgate Academy
    (B) A popular teacher who is leaving a school
    (C) Beth Morgan's teaching in London
    (D) A teaching job available in July

23. Why did Mr. Nathan send Ms. Bryers a letter?
    (A) To find a history teacher
    (B) To ask about the details of the job
    (C) To provide a recommendation for someone
    (D) To say he is interested in the job

24. What is one problem for Mr. Nathan?
    (A) He does not have five years of teaching experience.
    (B) He has never taught history before.
    (C) He does not have a recommendation letter.
    (D) He does not meet any of the requirements.

Shopping

Warm up　　　**Dictation Practice**　　　 2-61

それぞれの空所に入る2〜4語を、音声を聞いて書き入れてみましょう。

Attention, Central Bookstore shoppers. 1._____ 30 minutes from

now, the best-selling author Nancy Jones 2._____ a talk in the coffee

shop on the second floor. She 3._____ tell us about

4._____ decide to become a writer. And, also,

5._____ some 6._____ how to write clearer sentences.

Following the talk, she will sign copies 7._____ latest book,

8._____ available for purchase by the cash registers.

🔍 **Points to Dictate**

Part 4 形式のアナウンスの聞き取りに挑戦しましょう。店舗内で行われるイベントについて案内をしています。空所を埋める時には、音声だけではなく、前後関係や文法の知識も総動員して埋めるようにします。

✅ **頻出単語チェック！**　**Listening Section**

語句と意味を品詞に気をつけながら結びつけてみましょう。

1. try out [v.] (　　)
2. grocery store (　　)
3. shipment (　　)
4. inventory [n.] (　　)
5. supervisor (　　)
6. bulk discount (　　)
7. custom [adj.] (　　)
8. promotion (　　)

a. a discount given when people buy a lot of items
b. to use something to check it is suitable
c. a shop that sells food and other frequently used items
d. a delivery
e. an activity to help sell a product
f. a person who is in charge of other people at work
g. specially created for the customer
h. the items that a shop currently has in the building

Listening Section

PART 1　写真描写問題　 2-62, 63

Check Point!
人物以外と人物が主語になっている場合の代表例を見てみましょう。
There are some things in the basket.

それぞれの写真について、4つの説明文の中から最も適切なものを1つずつ選びましょう。

1.

Ⓐ Ⓑ Ⓒ Ⓓ

2.

Ⓐ Ⓑ Ⓒ Ⓓ

PART 2　応答問題　 2-64-68

Check Point!
付加疑問は肯定なら Yes、否定なら No で答えるのが基本です。
You read the final report, didn't you?

それぞれの設問の応答として最も適切なものを1つずつ選びましょう。

3. Mark your answer on your answer sheet.　Ⓐ Ⓑ Ⓒ

4. Mark your answer on your answer sheet.　Ⓐ Ⓑ Ⓒ

5. Mark your answer on your answer sheet.　Ⓐ Ⓑ Ⓒ

6. Mark your answer on your answer sheet.　Ⓐ Ⓑ Ⓒ

7. Mark your answer on your answer sheet.　Ⓐ Ⓑ Ⓒ

2-69, 70

> **Check Point!**　「何を要求しているのか」その内容を聞き取りましょう。
> What does the woman request?

会話についての設問に対し、最も適切なものを1つずつ選びましょう。

8. What does the woman request?
(A) A lower price
(B) A size chart for clothing
(C) A large shipment of items
(D) An item in a different color

9. What most likely will the man do next?
(A) Show the woman a catalog
(B) Speak with a supervisor
(C) Check the shop's inventory
(D) Call a clothing manufacturer

10. Look at the graphic. What percentage discount will the woman receive?
(A) 10%
(B) 15%
(C) 20%
(D) 25%

Number of Jackets	Discount
10	10%
20	15%
30	20%
40	25%

  2-71, 72

> **Check Point!**　話の内容と一致する部分を図の中に見つけましょう。
> Look at the graphic. On what floor will there be…?

説明文についての設問に対し、最も適切なものを1つずつ選びましょう。

11. Where most likely is the announcement being made?
(A) In a conference center
(B) In a shopping mall
(C) In an electronics store
(D) In a bookstore

12. Where can customers go to receive some free training?
(A) Courtyard Plaza
(B) Helen's Home Goods
(C) Wire Grip Electronics
(D) Skyview Plaza

13. Look at the graphic. On what floor will there be musical performances?
(A) The first floor
(B) The second floor
(C) The third floor
(D) The fourth floor

Directory	
Location	**Floor**
Courtyard Plaza	1st
Helen's Home Goods	2nd
Wire Grip Electronics	3rd
Skyview Plaza	4th

Grammar Review 受動態

受動態は動作を受ける人やものを主語にした表現です。

■**一般的な受動態**：通常、受動態に用いられる動詞は他動詞に限られます。また受動態は基本的には「be ＋過去分詞」の形で表されます。さらに動作主を by 以下に表します。

This desk **was made *by*** my grandfather.（この机は私の祖父よって作られました）

■ **by ～を付けない受動態**：次の３つの場合には動作主を表す「by ～」は省略されます。

1．The door **was broken** yesterday (by him). 話の前後関係から**動作主が明らかな場合**。

2．The building **was built** 50 years ago. 50 年も前のことで**動作主が分からない場合**。

3．English **is spoken** in the United States. 英語を話しているという**動作主が一般の人の場合**。

《例題》各空所に入れるべき最も適切な語句を１つ選んで、その記号を書きなさい。

1. All order forms ------- in duplicate.
   (A) are typed　　(B) are type　　(C) typing　　(D) type
2. The city is run ------- a mayor and 24-member council who were elected last year.
   (A) for　　(B) among　　(C) by　　(D) to
3. Many products currently on the market are ------- to last only a short time.
   (A) had　　(B) done　　(C) made　　(D) caused

Reading Section

✔ 頻出単語チェック！ Reading Section

語句と意味を品詞に気をつけながら結びつけてみましょう。

1. best-known (　　)
2. appliance (　　)
3. free shipping (　　)
4. combine (　　)
5. be sure to (　　)
6. stylish (　　)
7. additionally (　　)
8. exchange [v.] (　　)

a. a machine used in the house, such as a cooker or washing machine
b. don't forget to
c. delivery that you do not pay for
d. known by more people than other similar things
e. to change one item for another
f. trendy, fashionable
g. also
h. to use together with

> **Check Point!**　文法問題：受動態、語彙問題：形容詞
> 無生物が主語の場合は、まず受動態を意識しましょう。

それぞれの空所に入れるのに最も適切なものを１つずつ選びましょう。

14. The number of products that ------- at the store last year is higher than this year.
    (A) sell
    (B) were sold
    (C) are selling
    (D) have been sold
    Ⓐ Ⓑ Ⓒ Ⓓ

15. Customers ------- about several special offers on the company's Web site last week.
    (A) inform
    (B) informing
    (C) had informed
    (D) were informed
    Ⓐ Ⓑ Ⓒ Ⓓ

16. Sales at most clothing stores ------- to increase during the holiday season.
    (A) expect
    (B) will expect
    (C) are expected
    (D) have been expecting
    Ⓐ Ⓑ Ⓒ Ⓓ

17. Even though it was a Saturday, the shopping mall was not very -------.
    (A) crowd
    (B) crowds
    (C) crowded
    (D) crowding
    Ⓐ Ⓑ Ⓒ Ⓓ

18. Sue decided that the groceries were too ------- to carry home, so she had them delivered.
    (A) heavy
    (B) heavier
    (C) heavily
    (D) heaviest
    Ⓐ Ⓑ Ⓒ Ⓓ

PART 6　長文穴埋め問題

> **Check Point!**　語彙問題：形容詞
> 文章挿入問題：空所が文中なら前後と矛盾のない文を選びましょう。

それぞれの空所に入れるのに最も適切なものを１つずつ選びましょう。

Happy New Year from Harrison's

We want to wish all of our customers a Happy New Year. As you may know, this year is the 100th year Harrison's has been in business. Over that time, we have grown from a small store with just five employees to one of the world's ------- **19.** department store chains.

The great success we have enjoyed over the past 100 years is ------- **20.** to our wonderful customers. And so, as a way to say "thank you" to all of you, every product in every Harrison's store will be at least 10 percent off this month. That's right—every product in every store will be on sale. On top of this, the prices of some products will be reduced by as much as 50 percent. -------. **21.** So be sure to visit your nearest Harrison's store as soon as you can!

---

19. (A) full-time
　　(B) best-known
　　(C) up-to-date
　　(D) second-rate

20. (A) thanks
　　(B) thanking
　　(C) thankful
　　(D) thanked

21. (A) We will announce the sale soon.
　　(B) But this does not include large appliances.
　　(C) This sale cannot be combined with any other promotions.
　　(D) But the sale will only last until January 31.

> **Check Point!**　広告文とオンライン・ショッピングカートと E メール（3 つの文書）
> 3 つの文書の関係性を大きく捉えましょう。

文章を読んで、それぞれの設問の答えとして最も適切なものを 1 つずつ選びましょう。

New Suitcases Available Now

Yumonite is proud to announce the release of our Roll-Right Luggage Series. These suitcases are designed for frequent, international travelers that want to have a smooth, stress-free, and stylish traveling experience. Our Roll-Right suitcases come in four different sizes and are available in a variety of different colors. You can browse through each of these designs and colors on our Web site, *www.yumonite.com*.

*All suitcase purchases from our online store come with free express shipping and arrive in no more than 2 business days. Additionally, we offer free shipping on returns and exchanges.

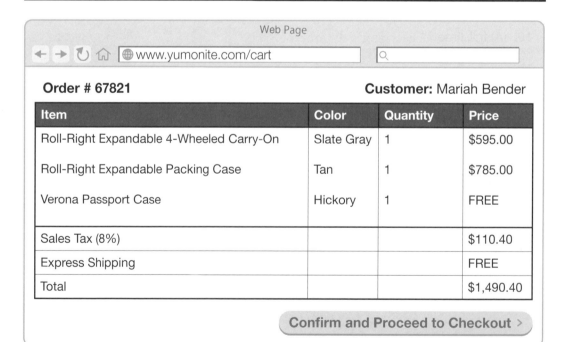

Web Page

www.yumonite.com/cart

Order # 67821　　　　　　　　　　　　　**Customer:** Mariah Bender

Item	Color	Quantity	Price
Roll-Right Expandable 4-Wheeled Carry-On	Slate Gray	1	$595.00
Roll-Right Expandable Packing Case	Tan	1	$785.00
Verona Passport Case	Hickory	1	FREE
Sales Tax (8%)			$110.40
Express Shipping			FREE
Total			$1,490.40

Confirm and Proceed to Checkout >

E-mail

To:	Mariah Bender <mariah.bender@trelkconsulting.com>
From:	Customer Service <service@yumonite.com>
Date:	October 11
Subject:	Re: Order #67821

Dear Ms. Bender,

Thank you for your recent purchase from Yumonite. It is my understanding that you would like to exchange your Roll-Right Expandable Packing Case for a different color.

You mentioned that you would like the replacement in Slate Gray, which you said looks very nice on the smaller suitcase. Unfortunately, this color is not available for our Expandable Packing Case. It does come in many similar colors, though. I have attached an image of each color option to this e-mail.

At your earliest convenience, please let me know which color you would like for the replacement suitcase.

I look forward to hearing from you soon,

Rhonda Hubbard
Customer Support Specialist

22. What is the purpose of the advertisement?
    (A) To explain a return policy
    (B) To introduce a limited-time service
    (C) To announce an upcoming event
    (D) To promote some new products

23. What does Ms. Hubbard indicate that Ms. Bender likes?
    (A) The color of her Roll-Right Expandable 4-Wheeled Carry-On
    (B) The size of the Roll-Right Expandable Packing Case
    (C) The selection available on the Yumonite Web site
    (D) The complimentary passport case

24. What does Ms. Hubbard request that Ms. Bender do?
    (A) Ship an item
    (B) Inform her of a preference
    (C) View the online catalog
    (D) Call a store manager

Education

:: **Warm up**　　　　**Dictation Practice**　　🔊 2-73

それぞれの空所に入る語句を、音声を聞いて書き入れてみましょう。省略形も含まれています。

Manager: Hi, Paul. 1._____ ?

Paul: Hi, Ms. Bachman. I'm fine, thanks.

Manager: Good. 2._____ today?

Paul: 3._____ visit two clients in the morning and then
4._____ ABC Bank at two o'clock in the afternoon.

Manager: 5._____ really busy. Before I forget, I
6._____. After you visit the clients, please
7._____ submit the report within three days.

Paul: Yes, I know. I was too busy last time to submit it
8._____.

Manager: I understand 9._____ company regulation. And it's
important for managers to know 10._____.

Paul: OK. I'll be sure to do that. Thanks.

🔍 Points to Dictate

Part 3 形式の対話文の聞き取りに挑戦しましょう。マネジャーと部下との
対話です。空所を埋める時には、音声だけではなく、前後関係や文法の知
識も総動員して埋めるようにします。

✔頻出単語チェック！　**Listening Section**

語句と意味を品詞に気をつけながら結びつけてみましょう。

1. point [v.] (　　)
2. seminar (　　)
3. enroll (　　)
4. signup date (　　)
5. placement test (　　)
6. evaluation (　　)
7. point out (　　)
8. semester (　　)

a. a judgement of someone's work or ability
b. a training or study session for a small group of people
c. to register for something
d. a part of the school year
e. a test that helps the school put a learner in the right level class
f. the last date that someone can join a course
g. to tell someone some important information
h. to use a finger to show people where to look

Listening Section

PART 1 写真描写問題   2-74, 75

Check Point! 人物以外が主語になっている例を見てみましょう。
The big clock is on the wall.

それぞれの写真について、4つの説明文の中から最も適切なものを1つずつ選びましょう。

1.

Ⓐ Ⓑ Ⓒ Ⓓ

2.
Ⓐ Ⓑ Ⓒ Ⓓ

PART 2 応答問題   2-76-80

Check Point! 平叙文なのに相手に返答を求めているものに注意しましょう。
It's hard to get a taxi at this time of the day.

それぞれの設問の応答として最も適切なものを1つずつ選びましょう。

3. Mark your answer on your answer sheet.   Ⓐ Ⓑ Ⓒ

4. Mark your answer on your answer sheet.   Ⓐ Ⓑ Ⓒ

5. Mark your answer on your answer sheet.   Ⓐ Ⓑ Ⓒ

6. Mark your answer on your answer sheet.   Ⓐ Ⓑ Ⓒ

7. Mark your answer on your answer sheet.   Ⓐ Ⓑ Ⓒ

> ***Check Point!*** 「何の問題が話されているか」その内容を聞き取りましょう。
> What problem does the man mention?

会話についての設問に対し、最も適切なものを1つずつ選びましょう。

8. What problem does the man mention?
  (A) He cannot enroll in a course.
  (B) His language level is too low.
  (C) He missed a signup date.
  (D) He failed an exam.

9. What does the woman mention about the test?
  (A) It will be held in a different building.
  (B) It will include a speaking assessment.
  (C) It will only be held twice.
  (D) It will last for one hour.

10. Look at the graphic. When will the man take his placement test?
  (A) Tuesday
  (B) Wednesday
  (C) Thursday
  (D) Friday

Course Name	Placement Test Date
Int. German	Tuesday
Int. French	Wednesday
Adv. German	Thursday
Adv. French	Friday

> ***Check Point!*** 「聞き手にどのような行動が求められているか」を聞き取りましょう。
> What are listeners asked to do?

説明文についての設問に対し、最も適切なものを1つずつ選びましょう。

11. Who most likely is the speaker?
  (A) A professor
  (B) A business owner
  (C) A financial manager
  (D) An event planner

12. What are listeners asked to do?
  (A) Tell each other a story
  (B) Complete the test
  (C) Update the schedule
  (D) Talk to Mr. Daniels

13. Look at the graphic. When will Ms. Valerie Potts give her speech now?
  (A) September 18   (C) December 1
  (B) October 14   (D) December 2

Schedule	
Guest Speaker	**Date**
Mr. Timothy Daniels	September 18
Ms. Valerie Potts	October 14
Ms. Delia Webster	November 2
Mr. George Wilson	December 1

✒ Grammar Review   関係代名詞

■**関係代名詞の格変化**：関係詞の格は先行詞に対して関係詞がどのような関係にあるかによって決まります。

●主格：Mr. Tanaka is a ***doctor***. **He** works for a big hospital.

⇒ Mr. Tanaka is a ***doctor*** who (=He) works for a big hospital. 先行詞 doctor を受けつつ、who 以下の節では主語の働きをしているので主格となる。

●所有格：Mr. Tanaka is a ***doctor***. **His** aunt is a famous movie star.

⇒ Mr. Tanaka is a ***doctor*** whose (=His) aunt is a famous movie star. aunt（彼のおば）とのつながりを示しているので所有格となる。

●目的格：Mr. Tanaka is a ***doctor***. I always rely on him.

⇒ Mr. Tanaka is a ***doctor*** whom (=him) I always rely on. 前置詞 on の目的語になっているので目的格となる。

《例題》各空所に入れるべき最も適切な語を１つ選んで、その記号を書きなさい。

1. I have a friend ------- runs a convenience store.
   (A) who   (B) what   (C) which   (D) whose
2. I know a girl ------- father is a famous dentist.
   (A) who   (B) whose   (C) whom   (D) which
3. She is the woman ------- I met at our office yesterday.
   (A) what   (B) which   (C) whom   (D) whose

Reading Section

✔ 頻出単語チェック！ Reading Section

単語と意味を品詞に気をつけながら結びつけてみましょう。

1. row [n.] (   )   **a.** worry
2. establish (   )   **b.** a date by which something must be finished
3. concern [n.] (   )   **c.** a line of something
4. attitude (   )   **d.** a way of behaving
5. extend (   )   **e.** positive feeling about doing things
6. enthusiasm (   )   **f.** to start a company or organization
7. participate (   )   **g.** to reach
8. deadline (   )   **h.** to join in with an activity

Check Point! 文法問題：関係代名詞、品詞：副詞
関係代名詞は、先行詞が何かを見極めましょう。

それぞれの空所に入れるのに最も適切なものを1つずつ選びましょう。

14. Mr. Andrews is the only teacher at the school ------- has lived overseas.
    (A) who
    (B) which
    (C) whom
    (D) whose   Ⓐ Ⓑ Ⓒ Ⓓ

15. Jane told me that the school, ------- was established in 1886, is the oldest in the
    city.
    (A) who
    (B) that
    (C) which
    (D) what   Ⓐ Ⓑ Ⓒ Ⓓ

16. The textbook ------- we used last semester is much more interesting than this
    one.
    (A) who
    (B) whom
    (C) what
    (D) that   Ⓐ Ⓑ Ⓒ Ⓓ

17. The students in the front row ------- raised their hands to answer the teacher's
    question.
    (A) quick
    (B) quickly
    (C) quicker
    (D) quickest   Ⓐ Ⓑ Ⓒ Ⓓ

18. Even though he only studied for a couple of hours, John ------- passed Monday's
    science test.
    (A) easy
    (B) easily
    (C) easier
    (D) easiest   Ⓐ Ⓑ Ⓒ Ⓓ

PART 6   長文穴埋め問題

それぞれの空所に入れるのに最も適切なものを1つずつ選びましょう。

Dear Mr. and Ms. Anderson,

It was a pleasure to meet you at the parent-teacher meeting last Tuesday. I'm glad that we had the chance to discuss your son Matt's academic performance.

-------. I share your concern that his grades are not as good as they were
　19.
in the previous year. But I don't think you need to worry too much about Matt. ------- he received a C on last month's math test, he is doing fine in
　20.
his other classes.

Another reason that I'm not worried about Matt is that he continues to have a very positive attitude about school and his classmates. You will be happy to know that his popularity ------- to his teachers, who love his
　21.
enthusiasm and sense of humor.

I'm confident that Matt's performance will improve, and I'll do whatever I can to encourage that improvement.

Sincerely,

Franklin Hawkins

---

19. (A) Matt is a student in my World
　　　History course.
　　(B) I have known Matt for three
　　　years now.
　　(C) Let's discuss his future again
　　　next time.
　　(D) You seemed concerned about
　　　his low test scores.

20. (A) Unless
　　(B) Whenever
　　(C) Even though
　　(D) Regarding

21. (A) will extend
　　(B) extends
　　(C) extending
　　(D) extension

> **Check Point!** 説明書とスケジュールと E メール（3つの文書）
> 3つの文書の関係性を大きく捉えましょう。

文章を読んで、それぞれの設問の答えとして最も適切なものを 1 つずつ選びましょう。

County Science Fair Application Instructions

In order to participate in this year's county science fair, students must submit to the following procedures:*

1. Complete the Application Form.**
2. Complete the Project Results Summary Form.
3. If your project is approved, then you will be invited to participate in the County Science Fair. You will also be assigned to a group based on your area of research:
   - **Group A**: Biology, microbiology, and zoology
   - **Group B**: Physics, astronomy, and chemistry
   - **Group C**: Environmental science and alternative energy
   - **Group D**: Engineering, electronics, and mathematics

*All forms and deadlines for each step in the application process can be found on the official County Science Fair Web site: *www.trdsciencefair.org*

**You will be required to submit: (A) your research topic, (B) your hypothesis, and (C) your testing and research plans.

County Science Fair Schedule

7:00 A.M. – 9:00 A.M.	Project Display Set-Up
9:00 A.M.	**Science Fair Opens**
10:00 A.M. – 10:45 A.M.	Group A Presentations
11:00 A.M. – 11:45 A.M.	Group B Presentations
12:00 P.M. – 12:45 P.M.	Group C Presentations
1:00 P.M. – 1:45 P.M.	Group D Presentations
4:00 P.M.	**Winners Announced**

✉ E-MAIL

To:	Melanie Albright <melanie@trdsciencefair.org>
From:	Samir Raju <samir.raju@bixcommz.net>
Date:	April 10
Subject:	Re: Science fair schedule

Dear Ms. Albright,

I would like to thank you for accepting my application to participate in this year's County Science Fair.

I just received the official schedule and I wanted to ask a question. On the day of the fair, I will be arriving by airplane, and I just learned that my departure time was changed. As a result, I will not be able to reach the Science Fair until 12:50 P.M. at the latest. I will still be in time for my presentation, but I will not be able to set up my project display in the morning. Is it all right if I have some friends set up my display for me?

I understand if this is not acceptable, but I hope that you will make an exception.

I am sorry for the trouble,

Samir Raju

22. In the instructions, the word "submit" in paragraph 1, line 1, is closest in meaning to
(A) agree
(B) present
(C) send
(D) write

23. What step is NOT mentioned in the instructions?
(A) Sending in an application
(B) Completing a survey
(C) Writing a summary
(D) Obtaining approval

24. What is the purpose of the e-mail?
(A) To report an error in the official schedule
(B) To request an additional application form
(C) To change a presentation time
(D) To get approval for a request

25. Which group does Samir most likely belong to?
(A) Group A
(B) Group B
(C) Group C
(D) Group D

TOEIC 必須複合名詞 100

1	☐	accounting department	経理部
2	☐	accounting firm	会計事務所
3	☐	additional cost	追加費用
4	☐	admission fee	入場料
5	☐	advertising agency	広告代理店
6	☐	advertising department	宣伝部
7	☐	amusement park	遊園地
8	☐	annual event	年間行事
9	☐	annual meeting	年次会合
10	☐	application form	申込書
11	☐	arrival time	到着時刻
12	☐	assembly line	組立ライン
13	☐	board meeting	取締役会議
14	☐	boarding pass	搭乗券
15	☐	branch manager	支店長
16	☐	branch office	支店
17	☐	bulletin board	掲示板
18	☐	business days	営業日
19	☐	business hours	業務「営業」時間
20	☐	business owner	事業主
21	☐	cash register	レジ
22	☐	catering service	ケータリングサービス
23	☐	CEO	最高経営責任者
24	☐	city hall	市役所
25	☐	conference call	電話会議
26	☐	construction worker	建設作業員
27	☐	contact information	連絡先情報
28	☐	company brochure	会社案内
29	☐	construction site	工事現場
30	☐	cost saving	コスト節約
31	☐	cover letter	カバーレター
32	☐	customer service	カスタマーサービス
33	☐	delivery date	配達日
34	☐	departure time	出発時刻
35	☐	discount coupon	割引券
36	☐	due date	提出期限
37	☐	eating habits	食習慣
38	☐	educational program	教育番組
39	☐	electronic device	電子機器
40	☐	entry fee	参加費
41	☐	executive director	事務局長
42	☐	expiration date	有効期限
43	☐	extra charge	追加料金
44	☐	extra work	超過勤務
45	☐	fitting room	試着室
46	☐	flight attendant	客室乗務員
47	☐	further information	詳細
48	☐	general manager	部長
49	☐	great success	大成功
50	☐	healthy food	健康食品

51	☐	home appliances	家電製品
52	☐	human resources	人事部
53	☐	identification badge	身分証明証
54	☐	information technology	情報技術
55	☐	job interview	採用面接
56	☐	job offer	仕事の口
57	☐	local news	ローカルニュース
58	☐	medical history	病歴
59	☐	medical treatment	医療
60	☐	membership fee	会費
61	☐	newspaper article	新聞記事
62	☐	office equipment	オフィス機器
63	☐	office supply	事務用品
64	☐	opening ceremony	開会式
65	☐	online form	オンライン・フォーム
66	☐	plane ticket	航空券
67	☐	press conference	記者会見
68	☐	price list	価格表
69	☐	price tag	値札
70	☐	public relations	広報
71	☐	public transportation	公共交通機関
72	☐	registration fee	登録料
73	☐	regular price	通常価格
74	☐	residential area	住宅街
75	☐	retail store	小売店
76	☐	return ticket	帰りのチケット
77	☐	road construction	道路工事
78	☐	safety inspection	安全検査
79	☐	sales department	営業部
80	☐	sales increase	売り上げ増
81	☐	sales manager	営業 [販売] 部長
82	☐	sales promotion	販売促進活動
83	☐	sales representative	販売員
84	☐	savings account	普通預金口座
85	☐	security guard	警備員
86	☐	shipping address	配送先住所
87	☐	shopping cart	ショッピングカート
88	☐	social media	ソーシャルメディア
89	☐	store owner	店主
90	☐	technical support	テクニカルサポート
91	☐	text message	テキストメッセージ
92	☐	traffic report	交通情報
93	☐	training manual	トレーニングマニュアル
94	☐	training session	研修会
95	☐	travel agent	旅行代理店
96	☐	travel expense	旅費
97	☐	user's manual	取扱説明書
98	☐	vice president	副社長
99	☐	work experience	実務経験
100	☐	work hours	労働「勤務」時間

TEXT PRODUCTION STAFF

edited by	編集
Mitsugu Shishido	宍戸　貢
Hiromi Oota	太田　裕美

cover design by	表紙デザイン
Nobuyoshi Fujino	藤野　伸芳

text design by	本文デザイン
Nobuyoshi Fujino	藤野　伸芳

CD PRODUCTION STAFF

narrated by	吹き込み者
Dominic Allen (AmE)	ドミニク・アレン（アメリカ英語）
Jenny Shima (AmE)	ジェニー・シマ（アメリカ英語）
Christiane Brew (BrE)	クリスティアン・ブルー（イギリス英語）
Jeffrey Rowe (CnE)	ジェフリー・ロウ（カナダ英語）

BEST PRACTICE FOR THE TOEIC® L&R TEST
—Intermediate—

TOEIC® L&R TESTへの総合アプローチ —Intermediate—

2022年1月20日　初版発行
2023年5月15日　第5刷発行

著　　者　吉塚　弘
　　　　　Graham Skerritt
　　　　　Michael Schauerte

発 行 者　佐野　英一郎

発 行 所　株式会社 成美堂
　　　　　〒101-0052　東京都千代田区神田小川町3-22
　　　　　TEL 03-3291-2261　FAX 03-3293-5490
　　　　　https://www.seibido.co.jp

印刷・製本　倉敷印刷株式会社

ISBN 978-4-7919-7253-1　　　　　　　　　　　　　Printed in Japan